The Shattered Synthesis

THE SHATTERED SYNTHESIS

New England Puritanism
before the Great Awakening

James W. Jones

New Haven and London, Yale University Press

1973

Designed by John O. C. McCrillis
and set in Baskerville type.
Printed in the United States of America by
The Vail-Ballou Press, Inc., Binghamton, N.Y.

Published in Great Britain, Europe, and Africa by
Yale University Press, Ltd., London.
Distributed in Canada by McGill-Queen's University
Press, Montreal; in Latin America by Kaiman & Polon,
Inc., New York City; in Australasia and Southeast
Asia by John Wiley & Sons Australasia Pty. Ltd.,
Sydney; in India by UBS Publishers' Distributors Pvt.,
Ltd., Delhi; in Japan by John Weatherhill, Inc., Tokyo.

To Sandra K. Jones

Contents

Preface   ix

Part One. The Seventeeth Century

    1. Background: John Norton (1606–1663)   3
    2. Giles Firmin (1614–1697)   32
    3. Samuel Willard (1640–1707)   54
    4. Cotton Mather (1663–1728)   76
    5. Benjamin Colman (1673–1747)   90
    6. Solomon Stoddard (1643–1729)   104

Part Two. The New Age: Puritan Liberalism

    7. Lemuel Briant (1721–1754) and Ebenezer
       Gay (1696–1787)   131
    8. Jonathan Mayhew (1720–1766)   143
    9. Charles Chauncy (1705–1787)   165
    Selected Bibliography of Primary Sources   199
    Index   205

Preface

The Puritanism that first landed on the rocky shores of New England was a synthesis of many elements. In ways that perplexed their own offspring as well as later commentators, the first generation of New England thinkers both believed in the absolute dependence of everything upon God and lived lives of incredible activity. They said man had no power of his own, and yet they forged new businesses, erected new colleges, and carved new cities out of the woods. They held in their hearts to an uncompromising faith in the objectivity of God's revelation and to a deep, vivid, subjective piety. During the antinomian controversy, strains began to appear. At the time of the Great Awakening these various elements broke apart into two camps—in the frontier pulpits one group hammered away at the absolute sovereignty of God and the importance of an inward experience of that sovereignty; in the drawing rooms of Boston the other group held forth on the importance of human activity and the objectivity of reason and conduct.

Histories often jump from the Antinomian Synod to the Great Awakening. It is easy to break off with Ann Hutchinson and Roger Williams and, with a glance at the Mathers, take up again with Jonathan Edwards and Charles Chauncy. The clash of personalities during the antinomian crisis and the distinct differences between Edwards and Chauncy are easier to trace and may be more exciting to read about than the sermons of Samuel Willard or Benjamin Colman. But to consider the Great Awakening or the rise of Unitarianism only in the context of the eighteenth century is to create two false impressions. It is to suggest that the split exemplified by Edwards and Chauncy was something new, when actually two divergent lines of development had been going on for almost a century before the first convert fell into fits of conversion on the floor of the Northhampton meetinghouse. The

Great Awakening did not create the controversy between those who demanded men be saved by breaking their volition over the anvil of the divine good pleasure and those who assured men that they could be saved by taking pride in the working of their wills. It only made the controversy public. To begin with the eighteenth century is also to imply that the humanism of those whom the Unitarians would call their forefathers was a new theme. Some have argued that it was something alien and represented the incursion of English and French rationalism into America. Actually the trend toward humanism was a dynamic within New England Puritanism and would have produced Chauncy and Mayhew without the aid of the Age of Reason. The Unitarians of the late eighteenth and early nineteenth centuries realized better than some of their modern sons and students that they were one half of a logical development from the Puritanism they rejected.

The Puritanism that was reverently carried across the ocean in the bulky volumes of divinity was a balance of the objectivity of the head and the subjectivity of the heart, of divine predestination and human activity. That balance was lost in the course of the seventeenth century; it was never regained. From then on American religious history has been, among other things, a warfare between those who proclaim the presence of God and those who insist on the morality of man as the essence of what it means to be religious. Some make rationality the only test of truth; others rely wholly on their feelings. What has become, in the twentieth century, the clash of a humanistic, scientific culture against a mystical, religious counterculture began in the pulpits of New England in the last half of the seventeenth century.

Many people besides the author made this book possible. The staff of the John Carter Brown Library went out of their way to supply ample material and pleasant surroundings. The trustees and administration of Macalester College gave me a one-year teaching and research fellowship that enabled me to do the writing. Mrs. Caroline Carlson's willingness to type and edit made the manuscript a reality. Professor Ernest Sandeen, chairman of the Macalester history department, contributed fruitful discussion and helpful comments on the text. To Sandra K. Jones I have already acknowledged my deepest thanks.

J.W.J.

Rutgers University
January 1973

Part One

The Seventeenth Century

1

Background: John Norton (1606–1663)

As John Norton sat in his study in Ipswich in October 1652, completing his treatise to be called *The Orthodox Evangelist*, almost a generation of New England's best theological reflection stood behind him.[1] Many of the founding theologians like Thomas Hooker and Thomas Shepard were dead; another, John Cotton, would die within the year. The so-called antinomian controversy that had set Boston against the rest of the colony and Cotton against the rest of the ministry had been over for fifteen years.[2] The issues it raised, however, still haunted Norton as he sat at his desk. In this controversy several Boston church members were fined and banished, and even their teacher, Cotton, came close to being condemned. The sum and substance of the controversy concerned the delicate balance between God's sovereign initiative and man's own role in the drama of conversion. The majority of the

1. Biographical data in the following section come from the *Dictionary of American Biography* (New York: Scribner's, 1957).

2. For information on this controversy, see Emery Battis, *Saints and Sectaries* (Chapel Hill: University of North Carolina Press, 1962); Everett H. Emerson, *John Cotton* (New York: Twayne, 1965); Perry Miller, *The New England Mind: From Colony to Province* (Boston: Beacon, 1966); Edmund Morgan, "The Case against Ann Hutchinson," *New England Quarterly* 10 (1937): 635–649. Norman Pettit, *The Heart Prepared* (New Haven: Yale University Press, 1966); Charles F. Adams, *Antinomianism in Massachusetts,* Publications of the Prince Society, no. 21 (Boston, 1894) and *Three Episodes of Massachusetts History,* 2 vols. (Boston: Houghton Mifflin, 1893); Larzer Ziff, *The Career of John Cotton* (Princeton: Princeton University Press, 1962); David Hall, *The Antinomian Controversy* (Middletown: Wesleyan University Press, 1968). There are also accounts in Cotton Mather's *Magnalia Christi Americana* and in Edward Johnson's *Wonder Working Providence* (New York: Barnes & Noble, 1959).

ministers, or elders, of the colony who stood against Cotton
said that the process of conversion was God's work and not
man's. But they felt Cotton and the antinomians went too far
in negating the human in favor of the divine.

Cotton himself almost shared the fate of his banished parishioners. For a while he considered joining his friend Davenport in New Haven and accepting voluntary exile. But fearing
to give outsiders the impression of colonial disunity, he decided to remain in Boston. In the fall of 1652, at the same
time Norton was preparing his magnum opus, Cotton rode
from Boston to Cambridge to preach at the college. He fell
in the Charles River and developed a severe fever. On No-
vember 21 he preached for the last time, and he died on De-
cember 23. Just four months before he died, he had penned a
preface endorsing Norton's manuscript, and on his deathbed,
he named Norton his successor.

A worthy successor he would prove to be. He would occupy
not only the same pulpit but also the same theological position
as had Cotton. Like most of the ministers who came to Massachusetts Bay, Norton had fled England to escape the hand of
Archbishop Laud. In 1634 he tried to leave England, along
with Thomas Shepard, who would be the pastor of the first
church in Newtown, or Cambridge, and would be instrumental in locating Harvard College there. But the ship was
wrecked in a storm, and the passengers narrowly escaped back
to England with their lives. Shepard successfully migrated
soon afterward, but Norton waited almost a year before trying
again. After refusing a pastorate in Plymouth, he was settled
as teacher in the first church in Ipswich. He was installed
just in time to take part in the Antinomian Synod.

The memory of that controversy, the deft replies of Mistress
Hutchinson, the endless arguing with Cotton in his stub-
bornness,[3] the fine theological points spun out like a thin

3. See the reports of the examination and trial of Ann Hutchinson in
Hall, *Antinomian Controversy* and John Cotton, *Sixteene Questions* and
Gospel Conversion. These two works of Cotton are repinted in Hall's
book.

thread and then woven together into a seamless robe of
orthodoxy with which the ministers tried to cover their differences—all of this must have been on Norton's mind as he
labored over his manuscript describing "the orthodox evangelist." This work has been called "an extremely technical exposition of the Puritan system of theology" (*DAB,* p. 573).
But mixed in with the endless points and subpoints, objections and answers (with even Cotton, in his preface to *The
Orthodox Evangelist,* admitted had the ring of medieval
scholasticism) was an attempt to piece together the theological
fragments of the first twenty years of colonial experience. This
experience had been shattered by the controversy surrounding
Ann Hutchinson, and now Norton was attempting to pick up
the pieces and place them together in a new configuration of
ideas that would heal and reconcile and express a ministerial
unity of consensus about the issues that had divided the
colony's ministers in its earliest days.

After the synod, Cotton must have realized that he was in
a minority. From then on nobody in New England held to his
complete rejection of the Puritan doctrine of preparation or
his emphasis on man's total passivity. Norton had been active
on the side of the majority of ministers, who had condemned
Ann Hutchinson and had quizzed Cotton carefully, if not un-
mercifully, about the fine points of his own position. As the
teacher of the church, Cotton was to be held responsible for
the opinions of the members of the congregation. But Norton
was obviously sympathetic to both camps. His manuscript
probably represented the best that Cotton could hope for. It
was far from a total vindication of the other elders or a whole-
sale rejection of what Cotton had stood for, alone, before the
synod of 1637. And so, having obtained Cotton's deathbed
blessing a decade and a half after the close of the synod, when
all the principals in the drama were dead and when he himself was in the midst of a controversy between Ipswich and
Boston as to who was to have the benefit of his ministry, Norton felt free to publish this act of reconciliation known as *The
Orthodox Evangelist.*

Norton's own thought and the shifts that took place in Puritan theology at the end of the seventeenth and the beginning of the eighteenth centuries had their immediate roots in the positions of both Cotton and the elders during the Antinomian Synod. Intellectually, the controversy revolved around Cotton's views on three theological points: whether the soul underwent any preparation before conversion or whether it was converted instantly, whether the believer's sanctification, his good works, could be any evidence that he was a truly saved Christian, and whether faith was an active or a passive state. Cotton rejected the elders' idea of preparation because he felt that conversion was the instantaneous union of the believer to Christ. Since one was either in union with Christ or one was not, there was no place in the process of conversion for a series of stages of preparation. Regeneration was analogous to *creatio ex nihilo*. It was instantaneous, without any antecedents. "To works of creation there needeth no preparation," Cotton reminded the elders at the synod.[4] Cotton fixed a gulf between faith and unbelief where the elders saw a progression of steps.

Cotton's concern was to safeguard the primacy of God's action and the centrality of Christ. He was afraid that if there were anything antecedent to conversion, it would encourage men to look to themselves to see if they were on the right track rather than waiting for God to work in them the overwhelming miracle of the new birth. The new creation was creation out of nothing not only because it was instantaneous but also because there was nothing in man, no stages of preparation, nothing he could do or say, that would influence this event. It was wholly of God and not of man.[5] The true Christian looked only toward the divine and not to any preparatory steps or stages.

4. *Gospel Conversion*, p. 2. Hereafter cited in the text of this chapter as *GC*.

5. *A Treatise of the Covenant of Grace*, p. 37. Hereafter cited in the text of this chapter as *TCG*.

The elders replied that they were able to preserve the divine initiative and the centrality of Christ without going to the dangerous extremes of Cotton's position. Just how dangerous his position was could be seen from talking to his pupil, Ann Hutchinson. The preparatory stages found in the believer prior to faith were just as much the action of God as was conversion itself. It is grace that works these conditions, the elders reminded Cotton; there is no danger of derogating free grace and the divine initiative, since these preparatory stages are "wrought by God's free grace." [6] These are not the actions of man, preparing himself for salvation; they are wholly the actions of God to bring man into union with Christ.

Unfortunately, Cotton could not accept this idea. He replied that this was still "popery" and quoted Bellarmine (a papist), who said that justification by works did not negate justification by faith, since the works were wrought by grace. Cotton said the true Protestant position was a complete distinction between the human and the divine, between works and grace. "In the Law, the promise is made to the condition or qualification of the creature, though given by God. . . . In the Gospel the promise is made to Christ." [7] In this sentence Cotton completely sundered the human from the divine. He identified the position of the elders, that God works in and through men, with the old law and with Romanism. He identified his own position, that God only works *upon* men, with true Protestantism. This was the heart of the controversy. The elders said men could look to Christ and acknowledge the divine initiative by looking at what he was doing in and through them. Men could look to God by looking to the works of God. For Cotton, men should not look at themselves at all, even at what God is working in them, but only at Christ.

This same concern inforced Cotton's understanding of the nature of faith. One of the questions the elders put to him, in their efforts to pin him down and find the source of Ann

6. Hall, *Antinomian Controversy*, p. 67.
7. Ibid., pp. 97–99.

Hutchinson's errors, was "whether Faith concurre as an active instrumental cause to our Justification" (*GC,* p. 37). It is clear that Cotton's position would forbid attributing any active power to man's faith. "If wee be active in laying hold on Christ . . . then we apprehend him before he apprehended us" was Cotton's reply to the question (*GC,* p. 39). From the fact that conversion was instantaneous Cotton could only deduce that men are justified "in the first moment of our conversion, before Faith hath put forth any act" (*GC,* pp. 44–45). Besides Christ, what need had men for preparation, or sanctification, or even the act of faith. Faith, then, was not an action that man performed but a state into which God brought him, the state of being joined to Christ. Faith is not the cause of men's union with Christ, it is that union itself (*GC,* p. 46). God apprehends men; men do not reach out and take hold of God.

Cotton argued before his flock that to say a man's faith was the cause of his justification was to deny the centrality of Christ. To make a man's faith the cause or condition of his salvation was to make faith a mediator between God and man. "Is faith then a mediator between Christ and us?" he asked rhetorically. "Can there be no union with Christ unless we bring faith and repentance with us?" (*TCG,* p. 217). Christ alone was the mediator of salvation, not faith or preparatory stages. To hold that faith mediates salvation to men, Cotton said, would be "popery" (the cardinal sin in Puritan New England), for it set another mediator in Christ's place (*TCG,* p. 218). To say that faith "be the cause of all the blessed gifts of God" would be to "deliver unto us another Gospel" (*TCG,* p. 33). Rather the centrality of Christ demands that men look only to him. "Take Christ and then you have all things in him" (*TCG,* p. 218). This indeed might have encouraged Ann Hutchinson's stance of total passivity and her claim that in the redeemed Christ did everything, man did nothing. The elders held to what they called an "instrumental" view of faith —that faith is, in some sense, an instrument or cause of man's salvation and not simply another name for the state of salvation. This meant faith must be seen as something active, something that causes, something that works. So deeply ingrained in the New England theology was this idea that faith was active and not passive that even Cotton was reluctant to say he believed in a passive faith although he certainly, in fact, did.[8]

Faith as the cause of justification meant that faith occurred prior to justification and effected it. Thus Thomas Shepard often said that men were saved "mediately by faith," [9] the very thing Cotton so vehemently denied. For Shepard justification by faith meant that faith was a necessary precondition and cause of justification.[10] For Cotton justification by faith meant the state of justification was equivalent to the state of faith. Although Shepard never failed to insist that faith was a work of God in man and not something man achieved on his own, he also said that faith is required of man as a condition of redemption.[11]

Peter Bulkeley went beyond Shepard.[12] Like Shepard he too denied that the natural man could receive Christ. He too insisted that faith was wrought in man by God. But he added to this the idea that what was created in man was not actual faith but a kind of faith in potential, what he called the "habit" of faith. God gave men this habit of faith, but man himself was responsible for acting on it. "God puts into us the habit of faith, and then requires of us acts of faith" was the way Bulkeley summarized his position.

These then were the difficulties Norton faced and the differences he sought to reconcile as he penned his manuscript. They were more than differences of thought or expression. Cotton and the elders represented two opposed ways of perceiving the relationship between man and God. For Cotton

8. Ibid., p. 44.

9. *Thesis Sabbatticae*, 1 : 117, in *The Works of Thomas Shephard*, 3 : 123.

10. *Short Catechism*, p. 43.

11. *Parable of the Ten Virgins*, in *Works*, 2 : 503.

12. See *The Gospel Covenant: or the Covenant of Grace Opened*, pp. 368, 369, 319, 333.

there was a radical distinction between creator and creature. Man must be totally abased before the sovereignty of God. For the elders the divine and the human need not negate each other, they could work together for the benefit of both. In this they were precursors of a more gentle humanism soon to become so much second nature to New England that some would, someday, take it for the original American Puritanism. Our task here is to trace this movement from the theology of divine initiative to the anthropocentrism of the eighteenth century.

Cotton and the antinomians insisted only on the strain in Puritanism that humbled the human in favor of the divine— a strain predominating in Hooker and Shepard as well.[13] The elders tried to balance this insistence with a commitment to the human side of salvation. They did not try to negate the divine in favor of the human, as some of their descendants would, but only to seek some balance between them. They tried to preserve the insistence on divine sovereignty but express it in ways that did not so totally exclude man's own role. They were great synthesizers. But in introducing into the stream of New England theology certain new models and concepts, they began the process by which the synthetic and balanced character of seventeenth-century American Puritan theology would be ultimately shattered by a more radical humanism than they could ever dream of. The place of the synthesis and balance would be occupied, in the coming century, by two warring camps—a more energetic and potent humanism and an even more radical and profound statement of divine sovereignty. This book is the story of how that synthesis broke down and how this state of conflict came about. It is a story

13. There are numerous references in both Hooker and Shepard to the need for man to be totally humbled before God and to have no will nor power of his own. For example, see Hooker's *Poor Doubting Christian Drawn to Christ,* and *The Soules Humiliation* bound with the *Unbeleevers Preparing,* and see Shepard's *The Sincere Convert* and *The Sound Believer,* in *Works,* vol. 1. This will become clearer in my discussion of Giles Firmin, who attacked Hooker and Shepard on this point.

that took shape beneath the pen of John Norton as he sat in his study attempting to reconcile the vision that must exalt God over everything else and the vision that must balance God's power with man's sense of his own selfhood.

Norton began his description of the orthodox evangelist in a very orthodox way: he started with a description of God. Although it was often customary in Puritan circles to begin a systematic discussion of theology with a discussion of man's knowledge of God, as Calvin did in the *Institutes,* Norton began with a definition of God. William Perkins and William Ames, two figures who did much to set the style and content of American Puritanism, began as Calvin did with the grounds of man's knowledge of God and the nature of that knowledge.[14] This was the way Thomas Shepard began his counterpart to Norton's treatise, which he called *The Sound Believer.* But Norton chose instead to begin with the order of being, with a definition of what God is, rather than with the order of knowing.

This was not simply a piece of pious sentimentality on his part. It was a way of emphasizing what he hoped would be the main point of his treatise—that everything begins and ends with God and not with man, not even with man's knowledge of God. The being of God was to be the principle from which everything else must be deduced and by which everything else must be justified. This was the context in which Norton would discuss those controversial subjects regarding the nature of faith and the process of conversion. The fact that the divine nature was the primary context of his discussion had a profound influence on his conclusions. The very organization of his treatise revealed that he shared Cotton's overarching concern for the divine primacy.

God was defined as "one pure and mere act."[15] His primary

14. Perkins, *The Golden Chaine,* in *Works,* vol. 1. Chap. 1; Ames, *The Marrow of Sacred Theology,* pp. 1–8.

15. *The Orthodox Evangelist,* p. 2. Subsequent citations of page numbers in the text of this chapter are to this work.

nature was not that of being or the philosophical ground of existence. Instead God has the character of action, of one who wills, who purposes, who accomplishes things. In short, God's essential character is that of sovereignty. God is God because his action, which is his very nature, is the cause of all that is. Norton's model of God was one of dynamism, activity, and total sovereignty. God is "the cause, and disposer of all things, the Antecedent and disposer of all events" (p. 51).

The elders had maintained against Cotton's strenuous objections that God worked conditionally. This meant that God did not decree everything directly. Rather, God decreed that some things came to pass on the condition that other things occurred first. Thus men were saved on the condition that they had faith. God's sovereignty over the total process was not lessened, since God worked the condition as well as the final outcome, the cause as well as the effect. The elders insisted that faith, necessary for salvation, was supplied by God. Hints of this model of conditionality can be found in Shepard.[16] Bulkeley maintained it was a consistency and forthrightness.[17] It did not undermine God's sovereignty, but it did mitigate the starkness of Cotton's vision of man's absolute dependence. It substituted order in the place of divine arbitrariness. Saying God worked conditionally made the divine modus operandi comprehensible to men. Some would say it even made God's ways predictable.

This also solved the major problem of Puritan theology— how to include human action within the scheme of divine sovereignty. God ordered not only certain ends but also the means to those ends. Men must use the means if they would obtain the ends. Since men such as Thomas Hooker insisted that the means did not work automatically, but only when God chose to connect means and ends, and Thomas Shepard insisted that God and not man supplied the means as well as the ends, this schema did not negate the divine predestination.

16. See *The Saints Jewel,* in *Works,* vol. 1.
17. *The Gospel Covenant.*

Hooker and Shepard never failed to remind their hearers that only the elect could use the means to any good effect. But this means–ends model, with its idea that God worked conditionally to bring his will to pass, did introduce into the body of New England theology a formula by which some would seek to bind and circumscribe the sovereignty of God in a new and more complete way.

This model of means and ends underlay, then, much of the elders' difference with Cotton. Since Norton shared Cotton's concern to maintain the sovereignty of God's will in its strongest terms, he too rejected the idea that God worked conditionally. Because God's will was simple and absolute, in other words because there was only one will in God, any distinctions in God's will or manner of working were invalid. This included the distinction between working directly and working conditionally. "The will of God is God by one, simple act, absolutely willing, the being of whatsoever he pleaseth. That distinction between the Absolute and the Conditional will [is] unfounded" (p. 17).

By simply dismissing the controversy over whether God acted conditionally, which had occupied so much of the debate between Cotton and the elders, Norton maintained the sovereignty of God in all its volitional nakedness. The will of God worked directly upon the cosmos to bring to pass his purposes. Thus everything that happens—whether it be an Indian raid, a storm, or a man coming to salvation—is the direct result of God's action. The elders would agree that everything happens by God's will, but they felt the need to express this in such a way as to account for man's own role in his redemption.

Yet there were problems with this direct approach to the divine sovereignty, even if one was not concerned to give man a part to play on his own behalf. The obvious problem was that of evil—particularly sin. Most Calvinists since Calvin himself had no trouble quoting the verse from Amos that asks, "Does evil befall a city and God does not do it?" They attributed directly to God's will many of the difficulties in the world on the grounds that these obstacles would eventually result in bringing his purposes to pass. But no one would attribute sin to the divine will, since, by definition, sin contradicted the divine will. Obviously sin must be ascribed to the human will. But how? The learned divines spent many pages trying to give man the responsibility in sin they denied him in redemption. Those, including Perkins, who had been most adamant in insisting that God's will was one and the same, his sovereignty ubiquitous and unrelenting, had to find some way to make an exception to all of that in the case of sin.

Most, Perkins among them, had recourse to the concept of "permission." [18] God did not directly cause sin, but he permitted it. Perkins was astute enough to realize that this idea of God's permission of sin was deficient in at least two respects. First, it implied that man could be a cause on his own, the very thing the attribution of all power and authority to God was supposed to deny. It made no sense to say God permitted man to sin unless man could in fact sin by his own power. If man could not sin on his own steam, there would be no difference between God's causing man to sin and permitting man to sin. And exactly this distinction had to be maintained in order that God not be the author of sin. But it was hard to maintain the distinction without making man a cause in a universe where all causality was ascribed only to God. Second, this idea seemed to negate the sovereignty of God by implying a distinction in the way in which God acts. Some things he causes, others he only permits. But the constant emphasis on the unity of the divine will and purpose undercut any such distinction.

Perkins tried to explain this subtle relationship between the human and divine wills in two ways. First, he implied that God did not negate or overrule the human will; rather he worked through it to bring his own purposes to pass. Second, he tried to maintain some balance between the idea of sover-

---

18. *Golden Chaine*, in *Works*, 1 : 15; *An Exposition of the . . . Creede*, ibid., pp. 156, 160, 294.

eignty and the idea of permission. Evil and sin do not take place, Perkins said, "by chaunce, or Gods not knowing of it; or barely winking at it or by his bare permission, or against his will; but rather miraculously, not without the will of God, and yet without all approbation of it." [19] Thus, in a sense, Perkins confessed he could not solve the problem. But he also did one very significant thing: he implied that however one understood the relation of the divine and human wills in the case of sin, this same model could be applied in the case of redemption. Adam sinned freely, yet within the sovereignty of God. So also, he said, men are redeemed freely, but by God's action.[20]

Norton confronted this problem in much the same terms that Perkins did. He suggested that God permitted sin for his own purposes, to bring his own ends to pass.[21] God's ordaining of sin was not "meer permission"; the decreeing of sin had a more active part than that in the divine economy (pp. 62–66). God's agency regarding sin was somehow different from his sovereignty in other areas of existence. God has a "mysterious Administration concerning sin, his foredetermining the being of it, his ordering the commission of it, his Governing of it to his own glorious end" (p. 66).

Like Perkins, Norton struggled to affirm that God can work through the human will without negating either his sovereignty or man's own volitions.

> God can determine the Will, and not prejudice the nature of the Will, because he is an infinite Cause. God de-

19. *Golden Chaine, in Works,* 1 : 19.

20. *Exposition of the Creede,* in *Works,* 1 : 159, 160; *A Reformed Catholike,* ibid., pp. 558, 560; *The True Gaine,* ibid., p. 661; *A Treatise of Gods Free Grace,* ibid., pp. 734–35; *A Commentarie upon . . . Galatians,* in *Works,* 2 : 178.

21. The fall was discussed under predestination in *The Golden Chaine;* and on the chart at the beginning of his treatise, Perkins directly connects the fall with God's decrees. God "hath most justly decreed the wicked works of the wicked," Perkins said (*Golden Chaine,* in *Works,* 1 : 15). Se also *Exposition of the Creede, ibid.,* p. 160, and *Treatise of Gods Free Grace, ibid.,* p. 724.

> termineth the will suitably and agreeably to its own na-
> ture, i.e. freely. He so determineth the will, as the Will
> determineth itself. . . . The Efficiency of God offereth no
> violence, nor changeth the nature of things, but governeth
> them according to their own natures. [p. 114]

There are two important points about this passage. One is the
idea that God treats men, and all creatures, according to their
nature and works on them in a way commensurate with their
own integrity. We will come back to this, for idea will have a
central role to play in our story. The second point is that by
suggesting that God works through man's natural agency, he
not only attributes to man an agency of his own but also comes
close to identifying God's will with man's nature inclinations,
the order of God's eternal determinations with the order of
natural causation.

This dilemma of wanting to give God causal efficacy in the
strongest sense while at the same time limiting this efficacy to
working through natural channels becomes clearer as Norton's
argument proceeds.

> The eternal, transcient, efficacious motion of God upon
> the Will, determineth the will with a real determination:
> the will so moved, moveth itself with a real, and formal,
> determination. . . . The Will placed under this deter-
> mining motion of God, inclineth itself freely to Act, and
> to that only where unto it would have inclined itself if
> . . . there were no decree. [p. 115]

Norton began by affirming that God alone had causal power.
Yet, in acknowledging that, in the case of sin, man too had
some agency, he was forced to try to bring these two wills in
line with each other. Thus he shared some of the elders' concern with the role of human agency in the drama of sin and
redemption. In a sense, perhaps because of the systematic nature of his work, he went beyond them. By bringing the divine
and human wills in line with each other, Norton tended to
limit the divine action to the channels of natural agency. In
nearly identifying God's willing with man's willing, divine de-

crees with natural causation, it would not be long before the divine and human wills were totally identified, making it no longer necessary to speak of the divine will at all. The human will, then, stood virtually autonomous, the divine will relegated to being only the background for man's own schemes and deeds. God's plan became identified simply with the state of the world as man understands it.

This final secularization and transformation of Puritanism into humanism will come only at the end of our story. The irony of Norton is that his delicate dialectics about the human and divine wills foreshadowed a time when the whole problem was resolved by a careless and perhaps naïve assertion in the eighteenth century that it was only common sense that man has will and freedom. Norton himself anticipated this carelessness about the problem when he could only conclude, at the end of almost two hundred pages of argument, that "man acts as freely, as if there were no decree, yet as infallibly, as if there were no liberty" (p. 199). In short, the divine determination seems to make little real difference in how men exercise their will since they act in the same way as if "there were no decree." It is the further irony of Norton's work that, in the course of attempting to reestablish Cotton's model of God's direct sovereignty against the elders' preoccupation with man's role, Norton opened the way for the ultimate demise of the idea of divine sovereignty and for a more complete anthropocentrism than any of the elders would have tolerated.

At first Norton's system appeared to contain a straightforward affirmation of the divine causality and responsibility in all occurrences. But the problem of evil and sin forced him, as it had his predecessors, to introduce an element of ambiguity into this scheme. The incredibly complex reasoning about the relationship between the divine and human wills that Norton used to make God the sole cause and yet give man responsibility for sin, could have been and was used to also give man some role in redemption (pp. 101–28). Neither Norton nor Perkins wanted to say that Adam's sin and man's redemption were exactly the same. In the case of Adam they wanted to play up man's responsibility and play down God's agency. In the case of redemption they wanted to play down man's responsibility and play up God's sovereignty. Yet in both cases some accommodation had to be reached between the human and divine wills. By implying that one case could be understood with reference to the other, it came to pass that as men grew more and more reluctant to ascribe sin to God in any way and instead gave the full responsibility to man, they did the same with redemption. And so in the eighteenth century, just beyond the borders of this study, those who came close to making God the author of sin denied that man could take any action on his own behalf. And those who gave man the total responsibility for his own salvation also made him alone responsibile for sin.

Obviously Norton's peculiar juxtaposition of the rhetoric of total divine sovereignty with the emphasis on the theme of human agency and freedom affected his discussion of the nature of faith. Like Cotton, Norton defined faith as the reception of Christ (pp. 250–51). He put the reception of Christ and not any preparatory stages or human actions as the first step in the process of conversion. "The Person of Jesus Christ . . . is the first saving gift actually applyed unto an elect person" (p. 249). No wonder Cotton, and not one of the elders, wrote the preface! This was the crux of Cotton's difference with Thomas Shepard and the rest of the elders. Cotton had said faith was the first and only step in conversion. The elders had said that preparation was the first step. Faith did not occur until after a man had been prepared for it.

In the heat of the controversy, Cotton had reminded the elders that faith must be seen only in the context of the divine election. Faith was wholly a function of God's "Effectual calling" (*GC*, p. 37). Norton, whose primary theme was the divine sovereignty, echoed Cotton. Justification was totally a result of God's decree, not of anything on man's part, not even man's faith. "Justification is actually procured, and hath its being in God's decree, and in our Surety, before we doe believe: Faith is no instrument or motive of Gods absolute decree to justify" (p. 231). Like Cotton, Norton rejected the means–ends logic of Puritanism and the idea that faith functioned as a cause of justification. The only cause of justification was God's election (p. 322).

> Faith doth not justify as a work. . . . God makes no account of faith which we account of as a work in the matter of our justification; the Believer is in this sense no worker. . . . to make faith as it is a work, to be part, or whole of our justification, were to make a Covenant of Grace, a Covenant of Works, and consequently to destroy the Gospel. [pp. 319–20]

It must have warmed Cotton's heart to read this because it is exactly what he had maintained against the elders during the synod.

The rejection of faith as a cause or instrument and the heavy emphasis on the divine election put Norton in the position, as it had Cotton, of affirming a passive faith. The title of one of Norton's chapters affirms that the soul is passive under the divine calling or vocation. When faith is infused into the soul and Christ is received, "the Soule is only a meer passive subject, and not in any way an efficient" (p. 259). It seems Norton went the way of Cotton, ignored the outcome of the synod, and refused man any role in the process of conversion other than to be a passive object of the divine power.

To have given man such a role would have been to subvert the whole basis of his work, which was, after all, to be a reconciliation and not only a vindication of Cotton. Norton solved the problem, as generations of Puritans had attempted to solve theological dilemmas, by making a distinction.

> Conversion is taken in a double sense, either for the immediate work of God, infusing a principle of life, and so regenerating the soule; this is properly Vocation, and in

it the soul is passive; or for the Life-act of faith, etc. whereby man being now converted, converteth himself unto God. [p. 271]

Thus Norton plowed up the ground that he had so carefully laid. This distinction between "Vocation" and the "Life-act" of faith is really a distinction between two stages in the process of conversion. First a man is called. As the object of this calling, man is wholly passive. But in the process of being called, man is renewed and made active. "In effectual calling man is altogether passive, being quickened and renewed by the holy Spirit, he is thereby enabled to answer this call" (p. 281).

For Cotton, man remained passive throughout conversion. For the elders, too, the natural man was dead in sin and could do nothing. But as men were being prepared, the Spirit was working on them to renew and activate them. This did not negate the Calvinist idea of man's inability to do anything to redeem himself, since only the elect received this blessing of the Spirit. Norton said the same thing: man may be passive when he is called, but he is very active when he has faith.

> The exercise of faith, or any other saving grace, is a life operation, flowing from the infused power, principle, or habit, through the help of the antecendaneous concurrence of assisting grace, in respect of which, the believer is not only a subject but also an efficient co-working cause. [p. 260]

What this somewhat scholastic definition boils down to is that Norton has let in through the back door what he shut out at the front. Faith may be passive and not a cause when seen under the rubric of effectual calling. But when seen in terms of the life-act of faith, man himself becomes "an efficient co-working cause" of his redemption.

The distinction between the habit and the life-operation was the same as Bulkeley's distinction between the habit and the act (pp. 260–62, 270–83). The soul may receive the habit passively, but then it becomes active on its own behalf. Norton relied on the same typology between Adam and the believer that the elders had used against Cotton. Adam, before the fall, was a type of the redeemed man. Since Adam had freedom and the power to act, so does man in the process of redemption. In the process of conversion the Spirit returns man to the state of Adam, active and free (pp. 268–83). Cotton, of course, rejected this typology. Norton utilized it, as did the elders, to show how man becomes his own agent in redemption.

Norton felt that as long as he saw the soul as passive at first, or passive in some sense, he would be free from Arminianism. After affirming that man is passive, Norton felt free to also affirm that man is very much alive and active. He spoke of a passive faith, but he allowed man a large measure of activity. Again he tried to maintain consistency by making a distinction.

> Passive is taken either absolutely, for that which is simply passive and in no respect active; so the soul is not passive, God doth not work savingly upon us, as upon stocks or senseless creatures; or it is taken respectively, for that which notwithstanding in some sense it be active, yet in some it is passive, the soul is passive in this latter sense. [p. 270]

The rhetoric is the rhetoric of Cotton, but the position is the position of Bulkeley.

Bulkeley said in *The Gospel Covenant* that the act of faith fulfilled the condition required of man for his redemption. For Bulkeley the covenant of redemption was conditional and faith was the necessary condition. Hooker and Shepard had not gone that far. Hooker had rejected the idea that the new covenant had any conditions; Shepard usually agreed. Sometimes Shepard implied that the covenant of redemption was conditional but then always added that God and not man must fulfill these conditions. When asked by Bulkeley to endorse his book on the covenant, Shepard played up (apparently because he felt Bulkeley ignored it) the idea that God and not man fulfills the covenant requirements.[22]

In his discussion of sovereignty Norton emphasized the unconditional nature of the divine will. God was no respecter of persons nor the activities of persons; the reason for his decrees was wholly his own good pleasure and not anything that man did. This obviously led Norton, as it had Puritans from William Perkins to Cotton and Hooker, to insist that the covenant too was unconditional. Only the elect will be saved. Redemption depends on God's call, not on man fulfilling any conditions (pp. 85–89). To say that faith and repentance (which Bulkeley and some of the elders took to be required of man as his part in the covenant) were conditions of redemption or causes of salvation would be "to change the Covenant of Grace into a Covenant of Works" (p. 228). Faith and repentance, said Norton, "are the effects of grace" (p. 228). They are not the preconditions of man's receiving grace but the result of his having received it. This was exactly the position of Cotton before the synod.

But Norton had also to allow for the position of Bulkeley and the elders. It would seem to be an impossible task. Cotton said that faith and repentance were the results of grace, not the conditions placed upon the receiving of it. Bulkeley said that faith and repentance were the condition of salvation required on man's part. Again Norton made a distinction.

> A Condition, is either a Condition properly so called (i.e. an antecedent Condition) Or a Condition improperly so called, ie. a consequent Condition. A Condition (properly so called) is a Law, or Observation annexed to a business; the performance whereof lyeth upon the Covenant. . . .

22. Hooker, *Unbeleevers Preparing, Poor Doubting Christian, The Covenant of Grace Opened, Christs Last Prayer* (London, 1640); Shepard, *Short Catechism*, p. 16; *Sertain Select Cases Resolved*, in *Works*, 1 : 317–19, 309; *The Church Membership of Children*, in *Works*, 3 : 521, "Preface" to *The Gospel Covenant*.

Such a Condition was Works in the first Covenant. If Faith were such a condition, there would seem to be an end of the Covenant of grace; yea, the Covenant of grace were indeed no Covenant of grace. A Condition improperly so called (or a consequent condition) is such a condition, whose performance by the covenantee, is absolutely undertaken for, and irresistably wrought by the covenantor, and not left in suspence upon the covenantee, to be performed by his own strength. Faith is a consequent condition, not an antecendent condition. . . . The condition of Faith depends not upon the will of the elect; either to be or not to be, but upon the absolute and gracious Will of God. [pp. 228–29]

As usual, Norton has reconciled both sides by taking the language of one side and the meaning of the other. In this case he took the language of the elders and gave it the meaning of Cotton's theology. The new covenant can be called conditional, but it is not a proper condition, which means it is no condition at all, since it is not up to man's will to perform it or not to perform it.

Norton, then, stood in the long line of such Puritan thinkers as William Perkins and William Ames, as well as Cotton, Hooker, and Shepard. All said the covenant was unconditional. Any condition there might be was fulfilled by God's grace and not by man's will. Norton saw that there were some in his time who adopted this position but turned it in a semi-Pelagian direction by saying that faith was the effect of grace but that it was a grace common to all men. To Norton, as to Shepard, the orthodox position was that faith was not only the effect of grace in a general sense but also was the effect of special grace, that is, of election.

The Pelagians, Semi-Pelagians, Jesuits and Arminians all affirm this proposition, viz. that Faith is the Effect of Grace. . . . The Pelagians understand by grace only the grace of nature . . . whereby the Will without any further help from supernatural grace is able to believe. Thus Pelagians confound nature and grace. The Semi-Pelagians . . . understand by grace the conjunction of supernatural grace with free will. . . . By grace, they [the orthodox] understand grace peculiar and proper to the Elect; therefore flowing from Election . . . in respect of which work, the soul . . . is meerly passive having no more causal power thereunto, than a dead body hath unto life. [p. 228; see also p. 230]

Norton, then, went beyond Cotton to affirm that faith was, in one sense, active. But he continued his predecessor's stress on divine sovereignty, election, and the unconditional nature of the covenant.

We have seen that Norton held Cotton's position that union with Christ was the first stage in conversion, which was what led Cotton to deny any idea of preparation. Norton, despite his attempt at reconciliation, followed Cotton. He did not avoid the question; one chapter is entitled "Whether there be any saving qualifications before the grace of faith." The same question was put to Cotton during the synod. He utilized the distinction between common and special grace to try to affirm and deny preparation at the same time. He begins with a distinction between two kinds of repentance. There was legal repentance, which goes before faith, and saving repentance, which comes after it. "Preparatory, or legal repentance, is a common work of the Spirit" (p. 154). Those who are under legal repentance are not under grace. But such legal repentance might dispose them to grace by removing certain impediments (pp. 154–55). This is a verbatim repetition of William Ames's position on preparation.[23] There are two kinds of repentance. That which is saving comes after faith and not before. Preparation and preparatory repentance are not necessarily effective but may partially dispose the subject toward salvation.

23. Ames, *Praeparatione peccatoris ad conversionem*, found in *Disceptatio Scholastica*, pp. 26–34.

More important than the genesis of this conception is the fact that Norton's distinction between two kinds of repentance mirrors his distinction between two kinds of grace. Common grace is given to all men. Those who are not elect participate in this kind of grace (pp. 170, 220). Special grace is given only to the elect. It is the lack of attention to this distinction, Norton said, that creates the confusion about preparation.

> The not distinguishing of Grace into common, and special or saving, troubles the understanding of the friends of Grace, obscures the doctrine of Grace, and advantageth the enemies of grace: Without it Pelagians, Semi-pelagianism Arminians, Papists, and orthodox, are all confounded together, for all acknowledge Grace. [p. 169]

Since "preparatory work is the effect of free, common grace" and "saving work is the effect of free special grace" (p. 139), this distinction allowed Norton to affirm preparation and to rob it of any significance. Preparation comes under the rubric of common grace, which all men have and which is not related to salvation. The saving work of God is a function of election and so has as little to do with preparation as common grace has to do with special grace, as little as the elect have to do with the reprobate.

Norton, then, agreed with the elders that there are stages of preparation that men pass through. But they may just as easily be passing through on their way to hell as on their way to heaven. Norton denied that preparation can be related to redemption "in way of causality"; preparation was understood "improperly" if it was taken "causally" or "instrumentally" (p. 139). In other words, preparation is not necessarily related to salvation at all. He affirmed that the elect may go through some preparation before they existentially receive Christ.[24] But as we noted before, the elect are saved long before they personally receive Christ, for they are redeemed by virtue of God's decree before the foundations of the world. Norton cut

24. See chaps. 6–7 of *The Orthodox Evangelist.*

the ground out from under the discussion of preparation by
suggesting that the real issue was not preparation at all but the
distinction between the elect and the perishing, between special grace and common grace. Whether one affirmed preparation or not was irrelevant; what was important was whether
one affirmed election in the starkest and strongest possible
terms, an affirmation in which he was one with Cotton.

Cotton, Hooker, and Shepard tended to ground redemption
in the work of Christ. Men were elected "in Christ," and the
nature of redemption could be understood by reference to
Christ. God's purposes in redemption could be read from the
events of Christ's ministry, death, and resurrection without
having to refer back to the hidden decrees of God lying
shrouded in the mystery of the divine good pleasure. Redemption had an existential immediacy because of the easy access to
the figure of Jesus in the New Testament. Rather than having
to become involved in a complex series of divine decrees and
counsels, rather than seeing redemption as simply the in-
evitable playing out of a prehistoric, transcendent divine decision, the plan of salvation became a drama, enacted in history, easily accessible for preaching and meditation by reference to the Christ event.

Norton, in his drive to see everything in the context of the
divine sovereignty, undercut this Christocentric image of redemption and located it instead in the realm of the transcendent divine decrees. He made a distinction between the efficient and the meritorious causes of justification (p. 304). This
was paralleled by distinction between election and the application of election (pp. 225–26). The divine will is the efficient
cause of justification; the work of Christ is the meritorious
cause. In the same way, the divine will is the cause of election;
Christ is the cause of the application of election. The effect of
both these distinctions was to ground redemption wholly in
the decrees of God rather than in the work of Christ. In the
first instance, the merit of Christ cannot justify men without
God's decree as its efficient cause. Although God could have

forgiven and saved men without Christ, simply by fiat, the merit of Christ could never save men without the efficient cause of God's decree. In the second instance God the Father chooses the elect; Christ comes in only as an auxiliary in applying this decree of election to individual men. So in both cases the work of Christ was demoted and the cause of redemption was pushed back behind the visible Christ into the invisible mystery of the divine good pleasure.

This move had two significant effects. In conceiving of redemption this way, Norton clearly articulated the so-called governmental theory of the atonement, which would become popular in New England a hundred years later. Second, as odd as it may sound, the way he grounded the work of Christ in the divine will paved the way for universalism, the heresy the governmental theory was adopted to combat. Again, it is the irony of Norton that in his attempt to reassert the sovereignty of God in a new way, he introduced concepts by which the sovereignty of God would be finally undermined.

First, his emphasis on sovereignty as God's essence meant that both sin and salvation must be related to divine rule. For Norton, sin was not an offense against God's honor (as Anselm implied) or the separation of man from the divine source but the frustration of the divine sovereignty or government. Since even the elect are sinful, they ought to die. But if they are condemned, election is voided. If they are not, God's justice (which, like election, is an expression of his sovereignty) is undermined. Christ steps in, pays the legal penalty, and allows God to forgive the elect. Norton sums this up in his book on the atonement, which carried out the principles found in *The Orthodox Evangelist*.

> The elect then having sinned, the elect must die; if they die in their own persons, Election is frustrate, God is unfaithfull; if they die not at all, God is unjust . . . if elect men die in their own persons, the Gospel is void, if man doth not die the Law is void; they die therefore in the

> man Christ Jesus . . . though God by his absolute power
> might have saved man without a Surety . . . yet having
> constituted that inviolable rule of relative justice . . .
> justice required that the Surety should die.[25]

Here then are the outlines of the so-called governmental
theory of atonement: its emphasis of retributive justice, the
idea that God by his sovereignty created a government or
moral order where justice demands punishment, the implication that Christ allows God to do what God really always
wanted to do anyway.

Second, the above quotation indicates a serious problem
with Norton's theory. He has so sidelined Christ and so tightly
tied redemption to divine sovereignty that the drama of salvation becomes more an expression of divine arbitrariness than
of divine love. Since redemption is wholly an expression of
sovereignty, "God by his absolute power might have saved men
without" Christ. God might have saved men simply by fiat.

Historically, the importance of this move is not so much
that it sidelined Christ but that it opened the door to universalism. Norton's distinction between the meritorious cause
of redemption (Christ) and the efficient cause (God's will)
meant that the work of Christ was dependent upon and con-
trolled by the will of God. That Christ's work did not save
all men was not a defect in the work but simply reflected God's
choice to save only a few.

> The Obedience of Christ is meritorious, not absolutely in
> itself but by vertue of the Covenant of God, accepting
> his obedience as meritorious. . . . The Obedience of
> Christ was of sufficient value . . . to redeem all mankind
> but it could not be a price, i.e. a ransom further then
> God was pleased to accept it. [p. 223]

Christ died for all men, but God chose to accept his death
only for the sake of the elect. Redemption was so tightly

25. *A Discussion of that Great Point in Divinity, The Sufferings of
Christ*, p. 4.

linked to divine sovereignty that only the arbitrariness of the divine will stood between Norton and the universalists. There was no limited atonement, since Christ's merit was sufficient for all. There was no need to refer again to the divine justice, since Christ had sufficiently satisfied the law for all men. Only the good pleasure of God prevented all men from being saved.

> The Merit of Christ being infinite, hath no bounds, but is extendible according to the pleasure of the disposer thereof, the obedience of Christ is all-sufficient, able to have saved the whole world, had God so pleased. [p. 325]

All that remained was for Chauncy to suggest a new definition of the divine good pleasure: that it pleased God to save all men, that God had more pleasure in redeeming men than in damning them.

Chauncy, of course, based his rejection of reprobation in part on the humanistic premise that man was intrinsically too worthwhile a creature to destroy. Norton, as one might suspect, was far from espousing this kind of anthropocentrism. But the distance from Norton to Chauncy may not be as great as Norton's ringing defenses of total depravity might suggest.[26] In his discussion of why a passive faith must be active in some sense, Norton said that God does not work on men as on "senseless creatures." Presumably in the case of inanimate or nonrational creatures, God simply moves them around. Taken literally the Calvinist doctrine of total depravity, with its emphasis on man's inability, his loss of his full faculties, his deadness, might imply that man too, at least when it comes to redemption, is a senseless creature and should be dealt with as such. Although William Perkins said that God worked through men's faculties without destroying them, he also spoke of man as a "tool" in God's hand.

Norton would have none of this. When he declared that man is a rational creature, he referred more to man's moral, than to his intellectual, capabilities. When it came to the intel-

26. See Norton, *The Heart of New-England Rent,* pp. 12–13.

lect, Norton continued to affirm with Calvin that there was
little of it left and that man's mind was in almost total darkness about spiritual things.[27] But what does remain after the
fall is a certain moral capacity, a good healthy dose of the
Anglo-Saxon, Puritan sense of duty. Man can still order his life
morally because his conscience seems less touched by the fall
than his reason. And so God does not deal with man as with a
stone or a cow but rather deals with him as a moral creature.
God appeals to his moral sense.

> The Rule of the reasonable Creature is the Moral Law.
> In the Government of the reasonable creature (one must
> observe) An Obediential power, That is a capacity of the
> Creature to become subject unto the Will of the Creator.
> . . . God prescribes unto the reasonable creature a rule.
> [pp. 103–04]

God does not rape man into salvation; He argues and persuades him. Norton had previously said that man was dead in
sin. How can a dead man be expected to respond to the call?
The Spirit comes and empowers man and puts him in a position where God can appeal to him and persuade him into
salvation.

> The Word calls upon us to will, and to do; the Spirit of
> Christ worketh in us to will and to do; the Word com-
> mandeth us to be according to our duty, the Spirit
> worketh in us to be according to the Word. . . . Man is a
> reasonable creature, therefore God proceedeth with him
> by way of Arguments: but because man is a dead creature,
> therefore he must work in him that which he perswades
> him unto. [pp. 212–13]

Since man is rational and moral, God deals with him by
means of commandments and summons to duty. Law and
gospel are brought very close together (pp. 212–13). Faith becomes obedience to the command to believe. Norton often

27. Ibid.

spoke of "obeying" the Gospel and often called the New Testament "the law of Christ." He said that the rule is the same "in both the law and the Gospel" (p. 211). There was always in Puritanism a tendency to understand the New Testament on the basis of the Old. Bulkeley made the new covenant a conditional covenant by paralleling it with the old covenant. Norton made the gospel a dispensation of duty and obedience, just as the old was.

Norton did not deny the doctrine of total depravity; as a matter of fact he constantly affirmed it in the strongest possible way. But this understanding of how God acts necessitated some new anthropological considerations. There must remain in man, after the fall, at least the basis for duty. There is still the light of nature, Norton said, which "consists in common principles imprinted upon the reasonable soul, by nature, inclining man to assent unto some natural and manifest truths upon the representation of them." [28] Man is in a position where God can present his duty to him and, empowered by the spirit, he can obey. As we trace the development of this idea, we will find God progressively adapting himself more and more to man's own nature, and we will find a continual expansion of the principles left in man after the fall, until the doctrine of man's depravity ceased to mean anything at all. By suggesting that God adapts himself to man to the extent of not dealing with man as with a brute creature, Norton opened up a little breach in the wall of total depravity. Through that breach would march the humanism of the eighteenth century.

28. *Heart of New-England,* p. 12.

2

Giles Firmin (1614–1697)

Far across the ocean, Giles Firmin too looked back on the controversy over preparation. Firmin had come to New England in 1632,[1] and, although he had studied medicine while in England, he was ordained a deacon under John Cotton. In 1638 the town of Ipswich gave him a tract of land in return for his medical services. Having sat under the preaching of Cotton, he now listened to Norton and carefully studied the writings of Thomas Hooker and Thomas Shepard. He married the daughter of Nathaniel Ward, "the simple cobbler of Agawam." [2] Ward, an opponent of religious toleration, also opposed the theology of preparation espoused by Hooker and Shepard because he said it demanded too much of men. Ward said the idea that, in preparation, men are to be separated from sin and humbled under the will of God is "to make men better Christians before they are in Christ than many are afterwards." [3] Firmin learned from Cotton and Norton, on one hand, and his father-in-law on the other, to reject the idea of preparation. Ward's objections were just the opposite of Cotton's. Cotton said preparation allowed man too much participation in his own redemption; preparation was too man-centered. Ward said it was too hard on men; it was too God-centered by demanding of man before conversion too much attention to the divine purity and sovereignty.

In 1648 Firmin left his wife and children to get along as

1. Biographical material on Firmin comes from *DAB*.

2. Ward's tract entitled *The Simple Cobler of Agawam in America* was published under the pseudonym of Theodore de la Guard and is a scathing attack on any form of religious tolerance.

3. Giles Firmin, *The Real Christian*, pp. 19–20. Subsequent citations of page numbers in the text of this chapter are to this work.

best they could and moved back to England, never returning to America. When he was called to a parish in England, his sympathies seemed to have been with the high-church Presbyterians or reformed Anglicans.[4] Apparently he was a royalist during the civil war, but he was later deposed for refusing to conform. He supported himself by medical practice and preached to a small congregation meeting in his home.

In 1670 he decided to publish his thoughts on the theology of preparation. He wrote them down in England but his targets were New Englanders, all of whom had been dead for over twenty years.

His work, *The Real Christian,* like Shepard's *Sincere Convert* and Norton's *Orthodox Evangelist,* was an attempt to describe the true nature of the Christian life. It was, like the works of his predecessors, a theological treatise and not a phenomenological study of Christian experience. In the introduction he explained why he undertook this work. The works of Hooker, Shepard, "and other such rigid men," he said, "have caused great trouble among Christians, who through the high respect they bear unto these men . . . have believed what they write must needs be the Truth of God." What was the trouble Hooker and Shepard caused? Their doctrine of preparation demanded too much, causing men anguish of soul if they could not find any preparatory steps in their own life. Firmin cited the story of a woman, who, after reading Shepard's books, "was so cast down, and fell into such troubles, that all the Christians that came to her could not quiet her spirit." [5]

The Puritan of the 1670s, it would seem, was not up to the spiritual exertions of the 1640s. Firmin came forward with a solution to this problem—adapt the standards to the new climate, lessen the demands in a less demanding age. Firmin, with his attack on preparation, was the spokesman for the "declension" of religion toward the end of the seventeenth

4. See *Presbyterial Ordination Vindicated,* pp. 1–2.
5. "Preface" to *The Real Christian,* unnumbered page.

century.[6] Although written in England, his work is both evidence for the declension and one solution to it; it was the solution finally chosen. The more theologically ignorant, morally lax, and spiritually weak the people became, the more it became necessary to be of "a charitable judgement." The more the fervor of regeneration waned, the more men decided that religious fervor was unnecessary if not unhealthy. The more men argued that all one could expect of "God's rational creatures" was correct knowledge and good behavior, the more inward regeneration became meaningless. So the land became filled with pious, upright, moral, but unregenerate people, for whom the name "half-way members" was more than an apt description. And so there arose a man whose judgment was even more "charitable." To consign to hell all these good but unregenerate people with which the declension and the half-way covenant had populated the land, Chauncy said, was preposterous. In a sense, Chauncy's universalism was the final stage in the process of adapting the expectations of the church to the declension.

Put another way, in Firmin's attack on preparation and what it signifies about the religious temper of the latter part of the seventeenth century, one can catch a glimpse of the forces that would give rise to religious liberalism in eighteenth-century Massachusetts Bay. The roots of the schisms of the eighteenth century lie in the state of piety of the seventeenth century. In those who began to adopt Firmin's outlook, one can find the seeds of the antirevivalist party of the eighteenth-century. In those in whose soul there lived an attitude opposed to that of Firmin, one can find the proponents of the Great Awakening. It would take two generations of theological watering before those seeds would sprout. It would take an event as cataclysmic as the shrieks and moans of the damned as they writhed under the preaching of Jonathan Edwards and George Whitefield to bring to the surface the divisions that

6. On the declension see Perry Miller, *The New England Mind: From Colony to Province* (Boston: Beacon, 1966)

had grown deep in the heart of Puritanism for almost a century. When Edwards and Whitefield called upon men to choose between Christ and Satan, they were also calling on New England to choose between the two different styles that had evolved in the heartland of Puritanism.

Each side of the controversy would claim to be holding to the faith of the founding fathers. Both sides stood in some continuity with the first generation and also within lines of development that had modified, each in its own way, the theology of the early seventeenth century. The Great Awakening did not so much create this division as simply reveal it; in Giles Firmin, one side appears to be taking shape.

The time that Firmin spent under the preaching of Cotton and Norton was not wasted. Although his main attack on preparation did not derive from either of them, in the rather wide-ranging barrage that he laid down against the idea of preparation, he borrowed much of their ammunition. Preparation demands that conversion be a process, but, asked Firmin, echoing the question that Cotton turned back upon the elders, "May not the Lord at the very first stroke convey an immortal seed of grace into the soul" (p. 18). Conversion may appear by abstract analysis to be a series of stages, but in fact Firmin said that all these stages "in order of time . . . go altogether" (p. 25). He agreed with the model of instantaneous conversion proposed by Cotton and Norton. He did not deny men the right to analyze conversion serially, but since this is only a schematic analysis and not a description of fact, he wanted to deny men the right to impose this schema on others as the sine qua non of conversion.

Since conversion is instantaneous, Firmin drew the same conclusion Cotton did. All true states of grace follow faith; they cannot prepare the way for it. "Those works which are called preparatory unto Christ, do most (if not all) of them, abide in the soul after its union with Christ" (p. 24). Therefore when a man undergoes these "works of God in his soul," he may think he is being prepared but actually he is probably already saved. Shepard and Hooker were too hard on men in telling them they are, at best, only being prepared for redemption while, in fact, they are already redeemed. Firmin, in rebuke to his former colleagues, said, "To say of a man under Gods working that he is but under a preparatory work, and no more, is a difficult thing" (p. 18).

But this was not where Firmin's heart really lay in his rejection of preparation. Actually he agreed that the soul must be disposed to faith before it can actually have faith. For Firmin this took place in three stages not unlike Hooker's and Shepard's stages of preparation. They were: first, illumination, where the soul becomes aware of its situation vis-à-vis God; second, conviction, where it realizes its sins; and third, compunction, where it loses confidence in its good works (pp. 107–49; see also pp. 45–48, 50–52, 56–69). In all this Firmin sounded like Hooker and Shepard, but he continued:

> Saith Mr. Shepard, between those preparations and Faith in Christ, there comes in one more to make up sound preparation. What is that I pray? The soul in that condition must lye under God, to be disposed of as helpless, quietly contented to lye still at his feet. But I pray, what mean you by this? that is, it must [be] . . . content, quiet, though God will never work grace, never manifest grace, never pity it, never help it, never succour it, never give it his love. In one word, saith Mr. Thomas Hooker, if the soul be rightly humbled, it is content to bear the state of damnation. [p. 108] [7]

For Hooker and Shepard the final and most important stage of preparation was humiliation. Here the soul must die to itself, look only to God, and be willing to be disposed of as God pleases.[8] Humiliation was the existential realization of

7. I have left out the page numbers referring to works by Hooker and Shepard contained in this quotation.

8. See the letters from Shepard referred to in the "Preface" to *The Real Christian* and on pp. 145–46.

the absolute sovereignty of God over life. It is often said that the controversy concerning a man's willingness to be damned broke out at the end of the eighteenth century with the theology of Samuel Hopkins. Actually this later controversy was only a reflection of the same issue from the previous century. This was what Firmin could not stomach. He did not really object to the idea of preparation per se. He himself suggested that certain things "ready" the soul for faith. But he constantly reiterated his opposition to this idea of humiliation. He constantly attacked Hooker and Shepard for demanding too much of man in asserting that man must be willing to be damned. He constantly recoiled from the idea of a God of naked sovereignty.[9]

Apparently Firmin corresponded with Shepard frequently over these points for he often referred to letters wherein Shepard reasserted the necessity of the soul's humiliation.[10] In one of these letters apparently Shepard gave two reasons for his emphasis on humiliation. First, "the advancement of Grace cannot be without the humiliation of the creature" (p. 115). Second, "Else the Lord should not be Lord, and dispose of his own Grace but a sinful creature will have the disposal of it" (p. 117). Obviously both these reasons were assertions of the absolute sovereignty of God. On this point Cotton, Hooker, and Shepard were all agreed.

Firmin first attacked the notion of such total self-denial by suggesting that it is impossible for men to bear the thought that God might damn them. Such an idea, he said, is too great a weight for the average Christian to carry. Only by special grace could one accept such a proposition (pp. 134–35). Shepard is said to have replied that it is not so hard, since Paul and Moses were willing to be damned for the sake of Israel. Firmin retorted that this could only be asked of such saints. "For a man to be so subject to the Justice and Sovereignty of God, that if he will deny him his love, work no grace, dispose him to damnation, he is yet quiet and con-

9. Ibid., chap. 5.
10. Ibid., "Preface" and pp. 117, 145–46.

tented" is beyond what is required of the ordinary Christian. It certainly cannot be required of men who are only preparing. Firmin quoted the remark of his father-in-law that Hooker asks a man to be a better Christian before he is in Christ than many can be afterward (pp. 19–20).

Despite their differences over faith and preparation, Cotton and the elders agreed on the importance of God's sovereignty. The elders sought to include within it an account of man's own role in conversion, but they did not seek to undermine or mitigate the divine sovereignty and initiative. This was especially true of Hooker and Shepard, as the latter's posthumously published dispute with Firmin shows. Firmin clearly felt that the idea of humiliation misuses, if it does not overemphasize, the divine sovereignty and initiative.

> The Lord is sovereign of his own grace, that he may have mercy on whom he will have mercy; we must acknowledge and tremble at it, though we know many men cannot digest it: but to teach that Sovereignty in this place, to a Soul under this work, brought now up to the great sense of want and high prizing of it, I think it is unmethodical. [p. 117]

Rather than emphasize the divine arbitrariness in order to humble a soul, Firmin argued that one should emphasize the more humane doctrines of God's mercy and forgiveness. "Sovereignty," he wrote, "doth not satisfy the appetite, in itself simply, it is no good for the will to possess, but the love of the sovereign God . . . this is heavenly food for the appetite" (p. 122).

Although Jonathan Edwards would "relish" the divine sovereignty as John Cotton and Thomas Hooker did before him, the naked sovereignty of God had become a load too heavy to bear. A lighter load had to be found. Because humiliation of the soul had become too difficult and inhuman a means to salvation, an easier and more rational way must take its place. But beyond that, when a theology was judged (as Firmin constantly implied it should be) by whether or not it satisfied men's appetites rather than the glory or will of God, Puritanism was dead.

The other assault that Firmin launched on the doctrine of preparational humiliation was based on an anthropological judgment that will be examined in more detail later. In brief, Firmin felt that it was man's nature to seek his own happiness; thus it was impossible for him to will anything contrary to his own happiness. To ask a man to aim at anything opposed to his happiness was, according to Firmin's logic, inhumane and unnatural.

> In all Gods Bible, there is not one duty that God requires of his creatures, which is contrary or cross to his creatures happiness. . . . This condition [humiliation] cuts off all happiness. First, it is contrary to man as man . . . to require such a duty as destroys the very nature of man, as he is a rational creature, it is most absurd to phansie such a duty. . . . It is determined by a natural inclination to its ultimate end, that is blessedness. . . . It is impossible for a man to will not to be happy; he must cease to be a rational creature in so doing. [pp. 141–42]

More important than Firmin's rejection of preparation was the way in which he argued. The idea of preparation was too deeply ingrained in the Puritan mind to be easily cast off and would continue, against Firmin's objections, for several generations. The nature of his argument, however, would carry the day. In suggesting that theological points should be decided on anthropological grounds, that doctrinal matters, even those most central to the Puritan schema, should be judged by their congruence with man's nature and not with God's will or word, he marked the beginning of a new day. In turning theology into anthropology and making man's nature the criteria for theological truth, he pushed Puritanism far along the way toward humanism.

The stages of preparation had ceased to express man's own

experience. As their diaries and biographical references indicate, men such as Perkins, Cotton, and Shepard were converted through the fiery furnace of total humiliation. The insistence on total divine sovereignty was, in part, an expression of the conviction that they had not come into the blessings of salvation until they had died to self and given themselves over to the divine will. Their preaching was not an abstract schematization of conversion but an attempt to recreate in each person's life what they themselves had experienced in all its terror and its joy. The generation that Firmin addressed, it would seem, could no longer find it in their hearts to humble themselves so completely before God. His book is replete with references to pastoral problems created when people could no longer bear the demand for such total self-negation. Shepard, firmly convinced that the steps of conversion were not rationalizations of the experience of his generation but were the truth of God's word, insisted that "we must not bring Rules to men but men to rules." Man's experience alone was of no value unless it correlated with the Bible. Firmin's reply spoke for a new generation, although he himself belonged to the old one. He did not primarily reply with a countering exegesis of Scripture but rather simply referred to the experience of men. Against Shepard's saying that men's experience must be judged by the word, Firmin said, "I appeal to thousands, and tens of thousands of precious believers, who never so much as heard of this dreadful condition, till these holy men printed it (p. 141). Hooker's cycle of sermons of preparation and Shepard's two treatises describing *The Sound Believer* and *The Sincere Convert* all presupposed that humiliation was the only sure way to come to God. Firmin believed that "the wayes of God in converting, or drawing the soul to Christ, are very secret, and in preparatory works very various" (p. 11). This was more than an appeal not to make one man's experience the test of all. It was also an indication of the fact that the old anatomy of conversion no longer expressed the experience and piety of the next generation.

His discussion of faith confirmed that the old way had become a stumbling block to people who were not up to its spiritual rigors. He attacked the Perkinsonian idea that true faith is the personal conviction that Christ has died "for me." For Perkins, faith was the same as assurance of salvation; it was the knowledge that one was indeed the object of Christ's atoning sacrifice. In Firmin's time, many were unable to come to such a solid experience of personal grace.[11] Faith, Firmin said, is simply assent to the gospel (pp. 182–203). It is an act of the will, not an experience in the soul, and therefore has nothing to do with assurance. Firmin was afraid that to require assurance as the sign of true faith (as Perkins did) would mean that the number of true believers would be very small—a possibility that did not worry Perkins (p. 201). Firmin was concerned with the lowest level of faith that is necessary (p. 206); Perkins was concerned with the highest degree of faith men could attain. When the least necessary and not the highest possible becomes the standard, Puritan zeal is clearly on the wane and the declension has set in.

Faith, then, is simply an act. Cotton's passive faith and Norton's actively passive faith have been left far behind. Firmin, extending Bulkeley's position, said faith was an act of the will that man performs (pp. 172–82). Firmin combined the active character of faith with the conditional nature of the covenant. Although some commentators have suggested that this is the essence of American Puritanism, it would have been abhorred by Cotton, Hooker, and Shepard. Cotton, Hooker, Shepard, and Norton all deplored the idea that redemption was conditional upon man's action. Even Bulkeley had to wiggle in the coils of his distinction between the habit and the act of faith in order to avoid the impression that the natural man could satisfy the condition of the covenant.[12] Firmin, however, could simply state that "faith is the great condition of the New Covenant of the Gospel, we are justified by faith,

11. Ibid., "Preface."
12. *The Gospel Covenant*, pp. 319, 332–33.

saved by faith . . . [a man is] justified, saved, by an Act" (p. 174). Redemption has become a contract: man must "come up to his terms and accept him" (p. 140).

Norton, a great proponent of the divine sovereignty, introduced into his system the idea that God works on man in a way commensurate with human nature. Firmin carried this even further and made it the crux of his rejection of preparatory humiliation. God must take account of man's nature, and humiliation is by definition the negation, not the support, of human nature. In all his dealings with men, God does not overwhelm them; rather, he appeals to their sense of duty and obligation, he persuades their intellect, he woos their heart.

> What the Sovereign God might have done with his Creature, I deny not; but it hath pleased him graciously to deal with man as a rational creature, giving him commandments. . . . He gives arguments suitable to them. . . . For my part I do not find the Scripture speaking after Mr. Shepards manner, who hath insisted upon nothing but sovereignty. [p. 122]

Firmin clothed the divine sovereignty in more humane robes.

Firmin was so determined to emphasize that God does no violence to man's nature that he outlined the steps of conversion in terms of the faculties of man. God must appeal to each faculty in turn, seeking to persuade or woo it.

> God in his working maintains the faculties of the soul in their actings, as he made them. . . . The day of his power is not a day of forcing the will, which cannot be done by even God himself, it must cease to be a will then. [p. 170] God in conversion or drawing to Christ works upon a rational creature, and works upon the soul as such. He calls the will and affections off from the objects to which they are glewed, to close with other objects: A reason for that, saith the will, and a sufficient, convincing reason too else

> you may call long enough before I will stir: the will is
> . . . a rational appetite . . . it must have one to lead
> and guide it, therefore doth the Spirit set up this light in
> the understanding first. . . . God preserves the workings
> of all the faculties of the soul, not the least violence is
> offered to any one in conversion; the will shall have as
> good reason given it to close with Christ as ever it had
> to close with its lusts. [p. 29]

Firmin not only has God dealing with man as a "rational
creature" but he has also put man in a place where he can
dictate to God. The picture of man's will demanding from
God sufficient reasons for conversion and of God being placed
in a position where he must appeal to man on man's own
terms is a far cry from the sovereign divine initiative that
Cotton, Hooker, and Shepard emphasized.

Like Norton, Firmin pictured God's primary appeal as directed to man's sense of duty. Since God has commanded men
to believe, men have a duty to believe and be saved.

> God calls me to Christ: it is my duty to go to him. God
> offers Christ to me, it is my duty to receive him, the high-
> est disobedience that can be is not to obey. . . . God
> promiseth me, if I believe in him, I shall have his love, his
> grace, be saved. My duty is to believe his truth and faith-
> fulness. [p. 145]

Men of Cotton's and Shepard's day, as well as Perkins and
Ames, felt that mankind was dead in sin and could not believe by its own efforts. For them the problem with the church
was that by holding out an easy way to salvation it engendered
hypocrites, men who thought they could have faith by their
own power. It would have been inconceivable to them to suggest that man has a duty to believe and if he simply does his
duty he will be saved. These men wrestled for months with the
power of God and the state of their souls and were often

driven to the brink of suicide in despair over their condition before they finally knew God's joy and peace.[13] They could not understand a process of salvation phrased in terms of man's simply doing what his natural duty requires. In Firmin, "the physician of the soul" has been reduced to a moralistic exhortator. Firmin replaced the fine discriminations of the inner life by which earlier generations of Puritans sought self-knowledge with a wholly external appeal: "It is the duty of all the sons and daughters of Adam to hear the Gospel preached, and Christ offered to them, to believe in, or receive Christ, be they prepared or unprepared" (p. 2).

Nothing makes clearer the tendency of Firmin's thought than his discussion of that central phrase of Puritan theology —effectual calling. The founding divines, following Perkins and Ames closely, defined effectual calling as God's effecting a new state in the soul. It was called effectual calling because it was irresistible and necessary; being a sovereign act of God, it did what it purposed. It irresistibly called men into salvation, but now that God must work "rationally"—which seems to mean nonirresistibly—the meaning of effectual calling changes.

> God works rationally upon the rational creature, suitable to its principles: if then you can make the soul see the object it feeds upon is really evil . . . and can shew it a better, so as the heart is convinced of it, then you may take it off. This doth the Spirit in the work of effectual calling. [p. 11]

Instead of the divine Spirit sovereignty calling men into election and infusing faith in them, the Spirit is reduced to trying to provide man with reasons to convince him it would be better for him to be saved than to be damned.

Since God does not coerce man into redemption, God is in

13. For a description of the conversion experience in the life of the early Puritans, see William Haller, *The Rise of Puritanism* (New York: Harper & Row, 1957).

the unenviable position of having to appeal to man. Obviously sin and evil are quite appealing and therefore God must "out-bid" the attractions of evil so that man will freely choose redemption. The process by which God redeems men, then, is like a country auction. God puts before the "will an out-bidding good, a pleasing sweetness" (pp. 177–80). God offers the soul the best possible deal, and, like a good New England merchant, it cannot resist.

Thus Firmin described conversion as a process by which Christ and sin haggle over the soul by offering it more enticing and attractive benefits. Conversion is not a rape or a renewing of the covenant but a bargain (pp. 175–77). "Thus it is Christ's out-bidding of flesh and the creature which strikes the main stroke" in conversion (p. 177). The omnipotence and sovereignty of God were constricted because they have no place in the process of conversion. Rather, God was put in the position of being kept waiting until man "deliberates, ponders, observes" whether redemption is really a better buy than sin (p. 244).

Conversion was described wholly in terms of the benefits of Christ. God must display his wares before a skeptical audience. Firmin had enough faith in man to presuppose, in complete opposition to Calvin, Perkins, and Ames, that man will naturally choose the good. Other Puritans had insisted that man's will was in such bondage to sin that it could only choose evil. But in order to make his scheme work, Firmin must assert not only that the will can choose the good but also that it will do so. If God presents himself in the most attractive way possible, man will naturally choose him (pp. 182–84). Firmin used the analogy of marriage as well as of the marketplace. When a woman becomes aware of the benefits of marrying a certain man, she will do it. In the same way, when the soul become aware of the benefits of Christ, it will choose him. God works on a rational creature by appealing to his self-interest.

I should reflect upon the infinite wisdom of God as if he
were not wise enough to know how to govern his Rational
creature . . . his design was to exalt his Love, Grace,
Mercy, Faithfulness, Truth and Goodness, which are excellent perfections in God, as well as sovereignty and Holiness. Therefore he is pleased to invite us, allure us to
obedience, by promises of great reward. [p. 307]

Earlier Puritans such as Perkins and Shepard had said that
man must love God and seek him for himself and not out of
any selfish motives. Perkins said that desiring salvation out of
fear of hell, clearly a motive based on self-concern, rather than
out of love for Christ was a sign of the reprobate. Shepard
had said that man cannot aim at his own salvation but only
the glory of Christ. Anything done from self-love was regarded
as sinful. Firmin argued that men can justifiably be moved to
salvation by fear of hell or the reward of heaven. Man can seek
salvation out of self-love (pp. 303–08). Firmin said it is not
necessary "to exalt that glory of his [God's] above our own
salvation" (p. 208); rather he identified what God wills with
man's happiness on man's own terms. "Never did God declare
against self, or call a man to deny himself in that which hind-
ers his own salvation and happiness" (p. 209). Thus Firmin
exalted self-love as a reason for coming to Christ (p. 218–23).
He went as far as to say that man need not love Christ for
himself but only for his benefits, that is, for those things that
appeal to man's selfishness (p. 212).

Already, in Firmin, the main lines of the movement from
Puritanism to anthropocentrism in the eighteenth century are
clearly laid out. Man could aim directly at his own salvation
rather than having to aim at the glory of God. Man's salvation,
now an end in itself and not a means to God's glory, was
identified with human happiness. Thus, Firmin made it possible for one's own happiness to be the goal of one's life. When
Samuel Willard implanted this scheme deeply in the theologi-

cal mind of New England, the trend toward a man-centered religion was almost complete, even before the century had turned. Puritan piety was dead. Puritanism had called upon men to deny themselves and aim at God's glory. That was the inner meaning of the doctrine of humiliation held by all the founding divines from Cotton through the elders at the synod. Firmin and the preachers at the turn of the century emasculated, when they did not reject, the doctrine of humiliation. They allowed men to exalt themselves and aim at their own self-interest under the guise of aiming at the glory of God.

In a sense we have come to the end of our portrait of Giles Firmin. We have seen his concern that theology be judged by anthropological criteria, and we have seen how this concern led him to constrict the divine sovereignty so that God could not work in any way that would be offensive to man's nature. We have witnessed how redemption, having been understood by analogy to the marketplace, was transformed from a process where man's will must be humbled and wait upon God's will to one where God's will must wait for man's will to decide on the best deal. We have seen man's baptism of self-interest as the natural and best motivation for his actions. But before we close this chapter, we must note a few subthemes in Firmin's presentation.

One is his reliance on the sacrament of baptism. In his attempts to rebut the view of conversion proposed by the "preparationists," he hit upon baptism as a model for conversion (p. 152). There had been, off and on, in Puritanism the notion of "federal holiness," that is, that the offspring of the members of the covenant are also in the covenant. Even Cotton came to accept such an idea at the end of his life although he distinguished federal holiness from election, thus robbing those federally holy of any necessary connection with salvation.[14] In their defenses of infant baptism, Shepard and Hooker also used a similar concept to give the children of church members

14. See *The Covenant of God's Free Grace.*

the right to baptism.[15] It was necessary to affirm infant baptism in order to keep the New England way, with its pure church ideal, from the charge of sectarianism. None of this was linked to a real sacramental view of baptism, that is, that the rite itself conveys grace. Like the Lord's Supper, baptism was not so much a channel of grace as a seal of the covenant. The sacraments testified to the fact that the covenant conveyed grace, but they themselves did not actually create grace.

For Firmin it was not so much that the covenant gave one the right to baptism but rather that baptism gave one the right to the covenant. Thus the sacrament itself became a means of grace. Perhaps this relatively "high" doctrine of the sacraments is not unrelated to Firmin's apparent sympathies for Anglicanism or high-church Presbyterianism. In any case, the fact is that for Firmin the sacrament gave one the right to the covenant. Thus the preacher was given a new basis to exhort and cajole the children of the declension, the children of the halfway covenant, those who were baptized but had not experienced regeneration. On the basis of their baptism, they could renew their covenant and so enter into salvation (pp. 123–24). We will trace this idea of covenant renewal, which made the experiential aspect of conversion unnecessary. It is probably no coincidence that this view of redemption by covenant renewal was coming in at the same time men were growing uneasy with the practice of requiring a recitation of conversion experiences for church membership. For Firmin the image of covenant renewal became the model for the process of conversion. Conversion was a simple act of the will to renew the covenant. The notion of experiential conversion that had nurtured the introspective piety of Puritanism was cast aside. The real Christian was one who decided, on the best of rational grounds, to choose Christ over the devil (pp. 244–49).

The whole brunt of Perkins's ministry had been that the

15. Shepard, *The Church Membership of Children,* in *The Works of Thomas Shepard,* vol. 3 and Hooker, *The Covenant of Grace Opened.*

baptized person was not necessarily the real Christian unless he had experienced some saving work in his life that conformed to the pattern of conversion. It was clear to Perkins, as it was not to Firmin, that many baptized persons were simply hypocrites and that men should be held to a stricter standard. The New Englanders had written this idea into their institutional structure when they insisted on a recitation of saving faith, according to the schema of conversion, as a requirement for membership.

But times had changed. Even Norton had been unsure whether the experiential tests for membership were valid. It was clear that as time went on, men were having more and more trouble discerning the works of grace in their lives. Firmin was adamant that conversion came in different ways to different people. He also rejected the schema of preparatory stages that had provided the framework in which the experiential tests were carried on and thus he concluded that the experiential test for saving faith was invalid. Men do not necessarily know the time of their "new birth," nor can they recite their experience in conformity with other's experiences (p. 13). Having been diametrically opposed to Shepard's statement that one must bring men to the rule and not vice versa, he now advocated changing the rule and standard of church membership to fit the men and women of the period of declension. The real Christian was simply one who had willed himself to Jesus, in baptism, without any experience.

Does all this mean that Firmin had left the Puritan fold and become an Arminian? In all fairness to him we must point out that he denied this was the conclusion to be drawn from his works but rather insisted that everything he said must be set in the context of election. Few, he said, will actually be saved, even under his more liberal dispensation. He attacked those "latitudinarians" in England who approached universalism or said that the number of the elect was larger than the number of the reprobate (p. 228). He also attacked Arminianism and said that every experience of conversion is another argument against Arminianism (p. 26). It was the furthest thing from his mind to deny election or move Calvinism and Arminianism closer together. He emphasized throughout that only God can convert men, they cannot convert themselves (pp. 26, 30–31, 287). He even sounded like Shepard and Hooker on humiliation when he said that in conversion "if God be great in thy heart, then the creature is little; and never doth the creature grow great in your heart, but God grows little" (p. 40).

But by Firmin's time the issue was not simply the affirmation that God converted man. As Norton suggested, even Arminians and Pelagians affirmed justification by grace in one sense or another. The dispute was over how God converts men. For Firmin, God did not convert men by causing them to be converted or by effectually calling them into salvation. Rather God appeals to man's own free will and self-interest. Man, it seems, had the central role in the drama of conversion. Firmin exhorted men by saying, "I am to attend to my duty, and look to him for his assistance" (p. 287).

In the preface to *The Real Christian*, Firmin reflected upon the rise of Socinianism, a form of Unitarianism that denied the divinity of Christ. But it was not the denial of Christ's divinity but the theological method of the Socinians that concerned Firmin. He put the problem succinctly when he said, "The Socinians make human Reason the Judge of all Theological Controversies." Firmin saw the Socinians as the advance guard of the Age of Reason that he feared was about to advance throughout the Anglo-Saxon world. Many Socinian books were already published in England, and Firmin warned New England that they could soon spread to the colonies.[16] Just as Firmin's book revealed that the declension was under way in New England, so its preface revealed that the Age of Reason was on its way to New England. Its arrival would force Puritanism to face new issues and regard old doctrines in a new light.

The movements we have seen from Cotton and the elders,

16. "Preface" to *The Real Christian.*

into Bulkeley, Norton, and Firmin had been almost totally within the internal dynamic of Puritanism. The arrival of the Age of Reason, with its emphasis on reason and nature, would force changes in Puritanism from without. More importantly, it would add impetus to those movements in a humanistic direction that we have noted were already taking place.

One such shift in the meaning of terms can already be seen in Firmin's preface. Previously, from the time of Cotton, Hooker, and Shepard through the writing of *The Real Christian,* the term faith referred primarily to "saving faith." All the issues surrounding the use of this term revolved around its role in the process of salvation. In the preface the epistemological issues involved in the use of the term faith came to the fore. In a sense this marks New England's entrance, theologically, into the modern period. The Socinians raised the modern epistemological question of how a man can claim to have knowledge of God. Questions about redemption were pushed into the background as the whole idea of man's knowledge of the God of the Christian revelation became problematic.

By and large the men we will discuss here did not confront the more radical questions about God and his existence. Even the most liberal New England theologian dismissed deism and the religion of nature out of hand. It was not really until after the Revolutionary War that New Englanders had to take more seriously the most radical claims of the Age of Reason. But simply because they did not become Socinians or deists does not mean that the people we will discuss did not alter their religion to bring it more in line with the Age of Reason. Whether this alteration came about by direct pressure from the new ideas, whether the Age of Reason just stimulated movements already under way in Puritanism before its full impact, or whether both were true may become clearer in the course of this study.

Firman, as well as many others toward the end of the century, stood on a boundary line. He discussed the issues in the

old terms drawn from classical Puritan theology, but he was
concerned in a new and stronger way to assert that God must
respect the nature and integrity of man. Since God's actions,
therefore, must be understandable by man, God's doings must
conform to man's reasoning. "All God's wayes are Rational;
what is irrational, or contrary to sound reason, cannot be imputed to his wayes" (p. 298). This moved him in a rationalistic
direction.

Firmin addressed an age in which piety had declined somewhat. Men no longer seemed eager for salvation.

> Blessed Lord, what mean these worthy men? Do we find
> the sons of men to be so eagerly set after thy love, after
> thy Grace, that we must now teach them, that they must
> be quietly contented and satisfied, if they suppose thou
> wilt never give them thy grace? How long may the poor
> Ministers preach and mourn at last they cannot get one,
> perswade not one in a year to care for thy love, to regard
> thy Grace. [p. 148] Do ministers now find that people are
> so eagerly set to seek their own salvation according to the
> Gospel? Do crouds of people come in so thick, that he had
> need to stave them off, and keep them out, with this
> puzzling notion? [p. 221]

These were references to Shepard, Hooker, and others who
propounded the doctrine of humiliation. Since men no longer
seemed capable of the old standards, Firmin's solution was to
lower these standards. The fewer people there were who could
produce evidence of regeneration, the less any evidence seemed
necessary. The more common right belief and good behavior
became, the more ministers came to expect only that. The
more morally ignorant people became, the louder became the
cry for more "charitable" judgments. In short, Firmin's solution to judge the rules by men, in opposition to Shepard's
maxim, took hold. The state of men and society became the
criterion for theological truth. Whether this practice led to the
decline of Puritanism or simply adapted it to the realities of

a new day, this principle was certainly subversive to the enterprise of Puritan theology. When man and his capabilities, rather than God and his demands, became the measure of thought, Puritan theology and the piety it nourished were at an end. When the "real Christian" was one who did what everybody could do, simply be baptized and assent to the truth, the distinction between the elect and the reprobate would soon vanish. Under this view of the process of conversion, election and predestination became meaningless, as did the way of perceiving the world as laying in absolute dependence upon God that they spawned.

3

Samuel Willard (1640–1707)

Samuel Willard [1] is the first person considered here who was raised in the colonies. Born in Concord in 1639, he was brought up under the ministry of Peter Bulkeley. He graduated from Harvard in 1659, where he was taught the standard theology of American Puritanism, and was called to the frontier pulpit of Groton, Massachusetts. It is a testimony to his ability that early in his ministry many of his sermons were printed and he became widely regarded. When Groton was destroyed by Indians, he was well known enough to be called to the Old South Church in Boston.

In Boston he obtained a reputation for heavy, scholarly sermons. Although he strictly maintained the prevailing orthodoxy in theology, he was liberal in his style. He welcomed Benjamin Colman, the pastor of the Brattle Street Church, which was founded in conscious opposition to the ecclesiastical influence of the Mather family. Colman had studied in England, where he was reported to have imbibed the ideas of English rationalism. Willard was also quick to relax the strict requirements for church membership based on a recitation of saving faith. He led the assault on the Baptists and the Quakers and also attacked the court that tried the Salem witchcraft cases, arguing against their methods and aiding the accused. When the charter was revoked, he advocated submission, but when Andros seized his meetinghouse and humiliated him and his congregation, he switched sides. He later preached a sermon against a hereditary or natural right of rule.

1. Biographical material on Willard is drawn primarily from *DAB*. I have also referred to an unpublished dissertation, "The Life and Works of the Rev. Samuel Willard," by George William Dollar (Boston University, 1960).

In 1700 he was made vice-president of Harvard. A year later President Increase Mather refused to comply with a new stipulation requiring the president to reside at the college. Mather preferred to stay in Boston with his friends and his pulpit and so forfeited the presidency. A controversy over who should succeed him could not be resolved and so Willard became acting president. For six years he ran the college while retaining his full duties as pastor of Old South Church. Being as orthodox as Mather, he probably did not favor the moves of Leverett and Brattle to expose the students to Anglican latitudinarianism. But he apparently got along with both the Brattle Street partisans and the Mathers.

In 1687 he began a series of public lectures on the *Westminster Catechism* that were given once a month on Tuesday afternoons. His reputation for scholarship and erudition was so great that, apparently, people came from all around the Boston area and from the college to attend them. He had delivered two hundred and twenty such lectures when, because of failing health, he was unable to continue after April 1707. He resigned his duties at the college in August and died on September 12. Twenty years after his death two of his students, Joseph Sewell and Thomas Prince, both supporters of the Great Awakening, erected his monument. In 1726 they published his Tuesday lecture series under the title *A Compleat Body of Divinity*. It was the largest book that had ever been published in the colonies, the first major folio size book printed in this country, and it took several colonial presses to print it.

The development of New England theology quickly moved beyond Willard. Even the editors hinted that *A Compleat Body* may have been a bit out of date when it was published. The same year it was published, Jonathan Edwards assumed his duties in Northampton. Five years later Edwards would ride into Boston and deliver the public lecture on *God Glorified in Man's Dependence*. And three years after that the first signs of the coming Great Awakening would break out in his parish. Willard's book was published almost on the eve of the awakening, but because the tide of events so quickly washed over and ran on past it, it has not been given the attention it deserves either by historians or students of theology. For historians it provides a complete (to say the least) summation of the theological development in New England during the seventeenth century. To students of theology it is as monumental a work as ever produced in the reformed tradition. It also shows the state of theology at the turn of the century, just before cracks would begin to appear in the Puritan synthesis with the emergence into the open of the Boston liberalism of Gay, Briant, Chauncy, and Mayhew.

Willard began with the presupposition that men naturally seek their own happiness.[2] The purpose of any discipline, he said, is to obtain certain ends. Theology is a practical study concerned with achieving a particular result. It is the queen of the sciences because it directs man toward his ultimate goal, which is his happiness, or "blessedness" as Willard called it (p. 2).

Having affirmed that man seeks his own happiness and that he can not, and ought not, be deflected from this goal (p. 7), Willard faced an obvious problem. Puritan theology said that man's chief end is to glorify God. Men like Cotton, Hooker, and Shepard, with their idea of humiliation, said that the law and the gospel divested man of his natural inclinations in the hope of bestowing on him supernatural ones. While affirming that men were indeed made happy in redemption, they set the glory of God against the natural man's search for happiness. As a reflection of the intellectual climate in New England at the turn of the century, Willard felt he couldn't simply negate this natural desire for self-fulfillment the way his predecessors

2. *A Compleat Body of Divinity,* pp. 1–2. Unless otherwise identified, subsequent citations of page numbers in the text of this chapter are to this work.

had. He must find a place in his system for man's drive for happiness, and he must define happiness in man's own terms and not in terms directly derived from theology.

Willard related man's striving after happiness to the glorifying of God by equating the glory of God with human happiness (p. 4). This meant two things. First, it was a way of reiterating the Augustinian theme that man, being made for God, is only truly happy in relation to God. Second, it implied that God is glorified in and through man's happiness. Although he denied that man's being happy added anything to God's glory (p. 5), God's glory and man's happiness were so interwoven that man could glorify God, not by seeking God's glory in itself, but simply by seeking his own happiness (p. 4). Previous preachers had used the glory of God to criticize man's selfishness and the self-seeking, acquisitive mentality of mercantile New England. Willard used the glory of God to baptize this same mentality. Men could now go their own way, seeking their own satisfactions, confident that they were also fulfilling their religious duties. Since there could be no conflict between the glory of God and human happiness, it was easy to assert that whatever makes for human happiness also makes for God's glory. Formerly men had said that human happiness is the by-product of seeking God's glory. Willard came perilously close to suggesting that God's glory is the by-product of human happiness.

This direction in Willard's thought is illustrated by his discussion of a controversial point of his day—whether or not a man ought to be willing to be damned for God's glory (p. 4). By applying the means–ends logic of Puritanism to the relationship between human happiness and divine glory, he made human happiness the means to the end of glorifying God. The glory of God was the chief end of life and yet men can aim at their happiness as a means to this end. The demand for total humiliation sundered this means–ends schema because it suggested that man should aim directly at the glory of God without any attention to the means to that glory, that is, human happiness.

> A Willingness to be Damned is inconsistent with a true
> Desire that God may be Glorified: Because it separateth
> those things which God hath made inseparable: It sup-
> poseth a clashing in that very Order, which God hath put
> between the End and the Means. It must therefore pre-
> sume . . . a Willingness to neglect the Duties to which
> the Promise is made. [p. 4]

Total humiliation put asunder what Willard had tried so hard
to join together—human happiness and God's glory.

It was the furthest thing from Willard's mind to encourage
men in their self-seeking. He insisted that any action that does
not serve God's glory is in vain, and he condemned the hypo-
crite "who pretends to aim at the glory of God, but really
makes Self his End (pp. 9, 10). But Willard made intention the
main consideration in any act (p. 9). Therefore a man can
seek his own happiness if it is with the intention of glorifying
God. No doubt it was easy to seek self-satisfaction and convince oneself that it will glorify God in the process although
Willard would no doubt condemn such hypocrisy. If the social
history of the period reveals an increasing concern with a
selfish acquiring of material possessions, it would seem that
Willard made it easier for that hypocrisy to flourish in the
minds of Boston's merchants.

No reader of *A Compleat Body of Divinity* can deny that
Willard's purpose was to affirm the divine sovereignty in its
strongest terms. He stood directly in line with the founding
divines, as well as with men like Norton, in his emphasis on
the total sovereignty of God and in his determination to consider everything within this compass. Everything that is, is subject to God's decree.

> The Decree involves every Thing in it, and hath left
> nothing uncertain as to that; It extends itself to all Effects

and Events. . . . And as it neglects not the Least things, so it orders the Greatest. . . . Yea, even the arbitrary contingent Actions of Reasonable creatures. [p. 102]

This decree allows no opposition or contingency; it "foreordains" and "pre-determines" everything that comes to pass (p. 102). Willard said, "There is nothing in the World that could have been otherwise, when all Causes are put together" (p. 135).

Newton's *Principia* was published in 1687, just four years before Willard preached these sermons defining God's relation to the world in terms of total causation. No dependence of the Boston preacher upon the British scientist is intended, but as the works of Increase and Cotton Mather reveal, the basic themes of the "new philosophy" were in the colonial air of Massachusetts Bay at the end of the century. Willard proposed the strictest idea of divine sovereignty by using the model of the universe as an interlocking system of causation governed by one "efficient" cause (p. 105). Saying that God is the one efficient cause did not mean that God directly causes everything that happens. Rather, God is the cause of the causal network that determines everything that happens.

Willard understood causation in terms of a power, or "vertue," by which the cause produces its effect. It is this vertue, which powers causation, that is God's action.

There is an Influential Vertue goes forth from Him with respect to the Entity which appears in every Effect. There is no operation of the creature wherein this vertual Influence doth not exert it self: hence all things that come to pass are Attributed to Him: no Creature could do anything at any time, if he did not derive the Vertue unto it from Himself by which it doth it. [p. 136]

God then is not the direct cause of all events; rather he is, so to speak, the cause-of-the-cause of all events. He is the ground of the cause–effect sequence, the power by which a cause produces its effect (p. 105). This allowed Willard to say that both the creature and God were causes of any act of the creature. But God's sovereignty is not an undifferentiated power: God not only powers all effects, he also foreordains and orders them.

Willard distinguished primary from secondary causation. God is the primary cause of something when he works directly to bring it to pass. One might say that in primary causation God is both the cause and the cause-of-the-cause. In secondary causation, "both the Being & Operations of Second Causes are from the First Cause Efficiently, yet they are the next Causes of their own Actions formally" (p. 136). One might say that in secondary causation the creature is the cause, and God is the cause-of-the-cause. The creature acts "formally" as a cause; God enables that cause to have its effect. This distinction will be of great importance when we discuss the relationship of God's sovereignty to man's own responsibility, for

> the Second Cause Acts, tho' Mediately, yet as Properly and Really as if there were no First Cause. The Being and Actings of the one, do not destroy the Being and Actings of the other; No, not in the very same actions: God Acts Efficiently and Influentially; the Creature Acts Instrumentally and Formally. [p. 136]

Thus Willard opened the possibility of both God and man being causes of man's redemption.

God expresses his sovereignty by governing his creation according to laws. Nature is governed by a law of nature implanted in it by the creator. God governs man as a rational and moral creature by giving him rules through which he can exercise his moral nature in choice and decision. (pp. 10–11). For man, this rule is not a natural law but is rather a series of covenants (pp. 10–11).[3] God could deal with men in a purely arbitrary way, but he chooses to deal with them by cove-

3. *Covenant Keeping the Way to Blessedness* p. 27 (hereafter cited in the text of this chapter as *CK*); *The Law Established by the Gospel, The Doctrine of the Covenant of Redemption* (hereafter cited in the text of this chapter as *DCR*).

nanting with them and thus respecting their nature (pp. 10–11). The covenants, then, are an expression of the divine sovereignty in relation to man.

All covenants, Willard said, are conditional. Like his former pastor Bulkeley, he insisted that "mutual obligation" was the essence of a covenant. He said of the new covenant, "To deny it to have conditions is to deny it to be a covenant" (*CK*, p. 10). Willard spoke of three covenants. The first, or old, covenant, made with Adam, was the covenant of works (p. 11). Willard rarely mentioned the Mosaic covenant and when he did, he tended to assimilate the Old Testament covenant to the New Testament covenant. Both are conditional; both are covenants of grace (*CK*, p. 9). This was very similar to Bulkeley's covenant theology, which identified the covenant of works with a covenant made with Adam before the fall. Bulkeley then identified both the Mosaic and Christian covenants of grace. This allowed him to keep the traditional reformed schema of two covenants and also make the covenant of grace conditional by patterning it on the Mosaic covenant. The fall made it impossible for men to fulfill the covenant of works, but it was still in effect.

For Willard, there were two covenants involved in man's redemption—the covenant of redemption and the covenant of reconciliation.[4] The covenant of redemption is made within the Godhead when Christ agrees to make atonement for the elect. After his work is complete, it must be applied to the elect. This covenant of God that applies Christ's work to the elect is called the covenant of reconciliation.

The covenant of redemption is the covenant of the atonement. For Willard the problem of the atonement was clear.[5] God expressed his sovereignty in terms of rule, order, and law, which man violated in the fall. Adam's sin then was a sin against the divine sovereignty, and restitution must be made

4. For Willard's covenant theology, see *A Compleat Body*, pp. 275 ff and the works listed in note 3 above.

5. For Willard's discussion of the atonement, see *A Compleat Body*, pp. 286, 339–40; *Covenant of Redemption; Law Established by the Gospel*.

to the divine order. Willard was sure that God might have promised salvation to men as an act of sovereignty (*CK*, p. 11). But since he has chosen to deal with man by means of covenants, he cannot do it. He must abide by the terms of the covenant. The old covenant said that if man sinned, he would be punished. Having sinned, man must suffer. Otherwise the divine sovereignty and order would be undone.

A way out is found. The terms of the old covenant can be fulfilled by a stand-in, or "surety," for mankind. Thus, in the covenant of redemption, Christ comes forward in the place of man and fulfills the requirements of the old covenant and also suffers the punishment due for the failure to keep it. Men are now on a new footing with God. They have, in Christ, both kept the covenant and suffered the punishment.

It is clear that this ingenious theory of the atonement is not unlike the so-called governmental theory. Sin is a violation of the divine order, not the divine honor or justice; so restitution must be made to the divine law, not to God's person. A way must be found by which the law can be upheld and men forgiven. Christ upholds the law by fulfilling it, and thus no dishonor is done to the divine government. "The Justice of God never sat in such state and majesty as when it arraigned, condemned, and did execution upon the Lord of Life and Glory. . . . God herein shows what a precious value he placed upon his own law." [6]

Now man must be brought to a position where he can enjoy this new status. So God enters into covenant with the elect to treat them as having fulfilled the law in Christ. This covenant of reconciliation, based upon the divine sovereignty, is made only with the elect (p. 14, see also *DCR*). And it is by an act of sovereignty that God chooses to accept Christ's sacrifices as a surety for man's own works. God could have refused to accept the sacrifice of Christ.[7]

6. *Law Established*, p. 22.
7. *The Fountain Opened*, p. 15. Hereafter cited in the text of this chapter as *FO*.

God the Father was not absolutely bound to accept any satisfaction at the hands of a surety. Had the Son suffered it, yet his Suretiship could not have been authentick but by the intervention of the Fathers voluntary consent. [*DCR,* p. 87]

In sovereignty God chose some to be saved. In sovereignty God entered into covenant with Christ to undertake their salvation. In sovereignty God accepted this work. And in sovereignty God applied it to the elect (*FO,* pp. 66–68).

In what sense then can these covenants be called conditional? Willard clearly wanted to maintain the rhetoric of a theology based upon conditional covenants. Besides making conditionalism the very essence of the covenant, he constantly reiterated that the new covenant of grace (which is the combination of the two covenants relating to salvation) has conditions. But by grounding the covenants in election, he removed any of the emphasis on man's own agency in redemption that was found in Bulkeley's and Firmin's ideas of a conditional covenant.

Willard had two ways of making the covenants conditional in theory and unconditional in practice. First, he said that all the conditions are fulfilled by Christ and not by men. "All the conditions which are thus required of you in the Covenant of Grace [are] firmly and faithfully undertaken for you by the Lord Jesus Christ" (*DCR,* p. 146). This position can be found in Perkins, Ames, and Cotton. The covenant can be conditional from God's standpoint and unconditional from man's. What God requires, Christ, not the believer, fulfills.

Willard also made a distinction between conditions that are antecedent and are causes or merits and conditions that are consequent and are the means to an end but not necessarily the cause of the end. God appointed certain means and ends to go together, but the means are not the cause of the ends. Thus faith and repentance are not called the causes of redemption but the "media" to redemption (p. 784). They are not condi-

tions in the sense of antecedent causes but in the sense of
states that concur with redemption. When God elects someone and calls him to redemption, he also supplies these media.
Willard never tired of insisting that only the elect are given
true faith and repentance. Since these gifts to the elect are not
antecedent causes of redemption, Willard can call them conditions of the covenant while robbing this idea of any anthropo-
centric tendencies.

> This will show us a satisfactory reason why many Promises
> come absolutely to us which are yet conditional promises
> in the covenant they belong to. The promise . . . comes
> absolutely to the elect, for they are converted without
> any previous condition in them. . . . Hence it is that
> through the Gospel he propounded so in the Covenant of
> Reconciliation as to Promise life upon Condition of be-
> lieving, yet God in faithfulness doth give to His Elect this
> Grace of faith, makes them believers against their natural
> wills. [p. 21] Conditions propounded in the Gospel are
> not anteceedent and Meritorious or so propounded as to
> be the procuring cause of God's love and favour . . . for
> whatsoever respected to price and purchase, we must refer
> it to Christ alone; but they are connex and consequent,
> only pointing unto the way in which the free blessing of
> Grace is to be obtained by mankind. [pp. 32–33]

Willard insisted with Bulkeley and the elders that the covenant is conditional. But, like Cotton and Norton, conversion
is absolute and unconditional.

Nowhere then is the drive to see everything within the
compass of divine sovereignty more clearly revealed than in
Willard's discussion of man's redemption.

> The first, original, or leading cause of this Restitution is
> his meer good pleasure. We are here pointed to the Divine
> Sovereignty, which in nothing appears more eminently
> than in this affair. . . . Some there be who do ultimately
> resolve into God's natural goodness, and that love which

he, as Creator, must bear to his creature. Others, who though they pretend to assign it to his Will, do yet seek a double Will in God, the one absolute, the other conditionate, and refer it to the latter, and hereupon do really make it dependent upon something in the creature. . . . Against all these . . . it was his meer good pleasure. [p. 250]

All the facets of redemption, the original idea, the work of Christ and the application of that work to the life of the believer, depend wholly upon God (p. 90). "Mans whole Salvation proceeds from God himself" (*DCR*, p. 133).

Sovereignty became the central category for understanding redemption (p. 253). "It is certain that the whole concern of mans Redemption and Salvation had it [sic] consideration and determination in Gods eternal decree" (*DCR*, p. 6). This meant only one thing for Willard, predestination (p. 254). God intends to save only a few whom he calls to salvation (p. 247); it is only for these elect that Christ died (*FO*, pp. 49–50). Willard denied that God elects some because he loves them and damns others because he hates them. All men are alike to God. In the same way, Willard denied that election is an act of mercy and reprobation an act of justice. Love and hate, justice and mercy, are finite categories and ought not to be applied directly to God. Rather, since God is absolute sovereignty, election and reprobation have no other source than his good pleasure. Nothing, not even the divine mercy or justice, stands above his sovereignty. Election and reprobation are not acts of mercy and justice, love and hate, but only acts of sovereignty (p. 260).

Willard said that God deals with man by way of covenant rather than by naked sovereignty because it is suitable to man's nature as a rational creature. Since the covenant was practically reduced to the level of naked sovereignty, Willard was ambiguous about the relationship between God's agency and man's responsibility. He wanted to maintain both the

strong sense of God's overwhelming sovereignty that his forefathers felt and the idea of God fitting his sovereignty to man's
condition that his contemporaries used to tame that strong
sense of sovereignty.

Over and over Willard iterated that man is a "cause by
counsel." This means he can deliberate, choose, and act (p.
124). Again, as in Firmin, the emphasis was not so much on
man's pure reasoning as upon his moral abilities to choose the
good and to act. Man as a rational creature is more man the
doer than man the thinker, more a moral being than a purely
intellectual one. We have noted Willard's distinction between
primary and secondary causation. God is a primary cause and
can work either directly or indirectly. Man is a secondary cause
—he is guided and preserved, directed and empowered, by
God's agency. Yet he also has what Willard called a "formal
principle" of action within himself (p. 143). Primary and
secondary causes "co-work" together. This, when combined
with the idea of a formal principle of action, would seem to
imply that man can cooperate with God. But this does not
seem to be Willard's meaning. Rather, he was always careful
to insist that God is the one who actually moves and directs
the actions of secondary causes. Willard often uses the example of a tool—God works through man the way man uses
an instrument (p. 143). This analogy does not give much actual
agency to man. Secondary causes have the formal principle of
causation but not the content, the appearance of agency but
not the substance.

Although he said that man and God co-work, when he
spelled this out it was always that God acts and man simply
moves. He insisted that man is totally dependent upon God
both for power and direction (p. 143). The first cause "leads"
the second causes. "The first [cause] must move before the
second can stir; the second depends upon the first and therefore *must be acted by it*" (p. 144, italics added). The first
cause is superior to the second. Men and God "are not co-
ordinate Causes, drawing together, but the concurrence of the

first is above and directive to the second. . . . As two master workman, equally undertaking a business, such are not the Creature and God. . . . [Men] are therefore called Gods hand" (p. 144). Finally, the first cause "determines" the second. God "guides and directs" men.

> The Eternal Decree of God, having fixt & determined concerning what shall be acted, and all the several circumstances of the Creatures operations . . . hence by His active Providence He must determine them. . . . Rational Agents are also determined it appears, because else there would not be an Absolute subordination of the Second Cause to the First. . . . He therefore makes them do what they do not mean. . . . They fulfill his determinate counsell [p. 144]

After listing all these ways in which the divine sovereignty seems to overwhelm any secondary agency, he went on to insist that men and God "co-operate." He said "there are some Natural Causes and some Free Causes." God does not "lay any compulsion or constraint upon free Agents; but all Second causes work like themselves. . . . Reasonable Beings act freely and according to their voluntary choice" (p. 144). This seems at best ambiguous. God does not coerce man as an external restraint on his freedom; rather, he works through man's own inclinations and will so that it is possible to say both God and man are the cause of man's actions. "The Sun shineth Naturally, and yet he makes it shine." In the same way man acts naturally but God makes him act.

Willard used the rhetoric of a theology of conditional covenants while denying that man can fulfill any conditions to qualify himself for salvation. In the same way he used the language of his contemporaries about man's being an agent while affirming that God works on his creation "by a sovereign Predetermination of all the actions of it. Rational agents as well as Natural come under this predetermination" (p. 146). The paradox of Willard's vision was that God uses man in such a way that man appears to be moving himself. Man is both a tool in God's hand and a causal agent of his own.

In attempting to balance the divine sovereignty and human agency, we have noted two problematic areas. The first was the fall and evil, the second was conversion. With his strong emphasis on sovereignty, Willard often appeared to ascribe evil to God's will.

He said that God often causes things that seem to be diametrically opposed to his will but that ultimately work for his glory (p. 134). Since all events are predetermined and foreordained, the tragedies that come upon man are a part of God's providence.

> God must be acknowledged to Govern all the Affairs of this world all the evils and calamities that break in upon men at any time, are of his bringing, both as to the things themselves, and the time of them, the Famines, Pestilences, and Wars which overtake a people and bring them low . . . are of his ordering.[8]

Man must submit to God's will in all things.

The paradoxical balance of divine sovereignty and human agency is seen in the fall. Willard stated that "God did certainly from all eternity foreordain the fall of man" (p. 178). Since the fall contributed to God's glory as the precondition of man's redemption, Willard said, "That mans Fall came within the compass of the Decree must needs be concluded" (*DCR,* p. 13). Hence he concluded that the fall was unavoidable but insisted that it was a product of man's free will and that God cannot be blamed for it. Since man is a "cause by counsel" he is responsible for the fall, although the decree "determined that he should do so" (p. 178). On one level this was clearly contradictory, but Willard in his paradoxical way was asserting that both man and God can be the cause of the same action.

This was even more true in the case of sin. He said that

8. *The Peril of the Times Displayed,* p. 72.

God's decree entails that sin "shall infallibly be" (p. 134). But God is not to blame. "Though God doth not approve of, but hateth sin, yet he saw it good, for an higher end, that there should be sin by his permission" (*FO,* p. 75). But Willard cautioned against using this concept of permission too loosely. "But we are not to think that Gods permissive providence is meerly passive . . . God hath certainly a hand in it [sin]." Yet he said, "It is blasphemy to charge God as the author of sin" (p. 203). Willard realized he was caught in a dilemma: he had asserted the divine sovereignty in as strong terms as ever heard in New England; yet he must not ascribe sin to God. The distinction between primary and secondary causation may help some. But in his effort to emphasize the divine sovereignty, Willard often collapsed secondary causation into primary causation so that secondary causation was just another form of primary causation. There are strong reasons why he must uphold ubiquitous sovereignty and yet deny God's authorship of sin. Finally, he can only confess it is a mystery and a paradox. "It is true, the way in which God doth this, is very abstruse and hard for us to comprehend; . . . we are to entertain it with humble admiration and not bold and fancy argumentation" (p. 203).

In the end, Willard reduced the problem to one of perception. The difference between primary and secondary causation, between God's sovereignty and man's agency, is a difference between two ways of perceiving the same event. "As an action comes from the Creature, so we are to reflect upon that in it; but as it comes to us, we are to look beyond the creature, to Him who doth all things according to His Holy Counsel" (p. 136). When a man does something, we are to give him the responsibility for his deeds. But when something impinges upon us, whether the actions of another person or the events of nature and history, we are to see them as God's actions. In everything that comes upon us, "we are to look beyond" to God, who is the one Power that stands behind all the kaleidoscope of forces pressing in upon us.

Thus it is much too simple to say that Willard so emphasized the divine sovereignty that he made man a puppet in God's hands, although he did refer to man as a tool. Nor can one say that he mitigated the divine sovereignty by making man a cause on his own. Rather, Willard caught a vision that he struggled to articulate in the words of a highly abstract system of theology. It was a vision of God working in and through men to bring his purposes to pass without negating man's will or the divine plan. Willard returned to these problems time and time again. *A Compleat Body of Divinity* is the record of a man struggling to do equal justice to man's intuitive perception of himself as an agent and man's profoundest religious perception of life as the expression of a divine purpose that cannot be foiled and that is sustained by a providential ordering of love and mercy.

The process of conversion also required that God's sovereignty and man's responsibility be brought into harmony. Again deeply religious issues were at stake. Christians from St. Paul to the present have perceived that salvation comes as sheer gift, as grace. Willard's heavy emphasis on election and the unconditional nature of justification did justice to the experience of grace as an unexpected and unearned miracle. In Firmin we noted the impetus of many at the turn of the century to take account of man's growing feelings of his own integrity and responsibility. This also seemed to involve giving man some role to play in his own conversion.

Willard constantly emphasized that God treats man as "causes by counsel," not as "meer machines which have no conception of things but as such who can consider and deliberate and chuse or refuse" (p. 781). In this vein, he sounded very much like Firmin.

> God deals with us in bringing us to this faith, according to our nature as Reasonable Creatures, by shewing us our object, and the fulness of sufficiency of it, by discovering

the terms of the covenant, on which we may come to be interested in it; by setting before us all incentives to move us to entertain it. [p. 51]

The reason God entered into covenant with man was that the covenant treats man as a rational creature (*CK,* p. 27). It sets before man reasons, arguments, and commandments in which he is free to exercise his deliberative and moral faculties. Like Firmin, Willard delineated the stages of conversion in terms of God offering to man "all Arguments persuasive to move him to comply with the offer made" (p. 431, see also 449–51). In the covenant, man is not raped into salvation but is given the chance to consider and choose.

Willard tried to balance his emphasis on sovereignty and this idea of man's rationality by distinguishing two kinds of conversion.

> We must distinguish between Passive and Active Conversion. This distinction is generally received among the orthodox. . . . Passive conversion then is that change which is made in us in Regeneration by the infusion of all saving Graces into us. . . . Active conversion consists in the exerting and exercising of these Graces. [*FO,* p. 131]

This parallels Bulkeley's distinction between the habit and the act of faith. In passive conversion, obviously man is passive—God works on him purely as an object of sovereignty by infusing him with certain graces. After this infusion, man is able to act and to be persuaded in the second stage, active conversion. "In the first infusion of Converting Grace into us, we are meerly passive. . . . Yet in Active Conversion, we are not merely passive but active and drawn with the cords of a man" (p. 781).

Willard realized that his contemporaries' idea of God treating man as a rational creature implied that man is such a creature. The doctrine of original sin entails that man has no power to be active in his conversion. This dilemma can be solved only by positing a "habit of faith" on the basis of which man can act.

> The means are properly accommodated to work of man as a moral agent. . . . But either their operation is common, and that can at most be but preparatory; or it is saving, and then it supposeth this habit in them. Moral suasion can do only on a subject capable. Some to the grave of a dead man, and make never so grave an oration over him, tell him what a miserable condition a state of Death is, and what benefits accompany the living, and so beg of him to rise and live; and what will this do? There must be Faith. [p. 434]

The natural man is a dead man. Appeals, like Firmin's, to moral arguments achieve nothing. The infusion of the habit of faith creates a halfway state between being dead and being alive. On the basis of this habit, man can be addressed and persuaded.

This distinction, then, allowed Willard to make two kinds of statements. Statements about man's inability and the necessity for the imposition of God's sovereign action are referred to man before the habit of faith is infused. These kinds of statements refer to passive conversion. Statements about man as a rational creature and God treating him as such refer to man after this habit has been infused. They refer to active conversion. As time progressed men began to feel both a lessening of commitment to God's absolute sovereignty and a conviction that the doctrine of original sin went too far. These men had no need for the first kind of statements, and so only the second remained. The only kind of conversion they preached was active conversion based on moral persuasion.

Bulkeley implied that after the habit was infused, man could, in some sense, act on his own. The elders maintained something similar at the synod by suggesting that God worked on man by setting in motion man's own abilities to act.[9] Cotton objected that each action of the believer was just as much an action of God upon him as the beginning of conversion. Although following Bulkeley in his distinction between the habit and the act, Willard did not go as far as his old pastor in attributing any ability to man. The act of faith is not really an act at all in the sense of something man does. Rather, the act of faith is something that the Spirit draws forth from man (p. 443).[10] Even after the habit of faith, man still must be worked on by God. Willard said that man cooperates in bringing forth this act, but it is the cooperation of the secondary cause with the primary agent (pp. 458–59). Man acts, but he acts as an "instrument of the Spirit"; man has a principle of action in himself, but it can only function as the Spirit works through it (p. 459). In short, man's role in conversion is the same role noted throughout Willard's writings, particularly in the relationship of primary to secondary causes. Man acts but he only acts as the sovereignty of God works through him.

It is clear from his writings and those of his contemporaries that Willard lived at a time when men were becoming cognizant of themselves in a new way as moral creatures. It is also clear that the end of the century was a time of declining religious zeal. Willard decried the increasing formalism and deadness of his age with as much vigor as any other preacher.[11] He also felt that there was a connection between the new concern for man's moral agency and the growing spiritual lethargy. He

9. David Hall, *The Antinomian Controversy* (Middletown: Wesleyan University Press, 1968), pp. 143–45.

10. William Ames, too, said that active faith was an "Actus elicitus" (*The Marrow of Sacred Theology*, p. 113), that it is something drawn forth from man rather than performed by him.

11. See *The Fountain Opened, The Peril of the Times Displayed, Morality not to be Relied upon for Life* (hereafter cited in the text of this chapter as *MNR*), *The Duty of a People that have Renewed their Covenant with God*.

strived to take account of the new themes, but he always returned to the overpowering sovereignty of God, which he saw as the foundation of the livelier piety of past ages. His delicate, and perhaps oversubtle, attempts to reconcile man's agency and God's sovereignty were his contribution to keeping the new trend within manageable limits. Man may be a cause, but he is still only a secondary one. God alone remains primary.

Willard was forthright in warning men of the dangers inherent in the new concern with man as a moral being. In his sermon "Morality not to be relied on for Life," he launched an attack on what he called "the moralist." [12] The moralist was one who said that man's morality alone was sufficient for salvation—the good man was the redeemed man. This sermon, preached and published right at the turn of the century, was an omen of things to come. Just the fact that he must assert, against an obviously growing body of opinion, that "meer morality will leave the man shut out of Eternal Life and under the curse of Eternal Death" (*MNR*, p. 15) said much about the direction Puritanism traveled in the course of the seventeenth century.

> The legal moralist is not only a stranger to, but an enemy of this faith. He acknowledgeth nother faith but one that is Historical, and is contained in the assent given to the articles of religion. . . . He hath a righteousness of his own which he sets up in contradiction to the righteousness of faith. [*MNR*, p. 25]

Obviously there were many such "legal moralists" in Boston, and the next century would see many more.

The irony of Willard is that his practice gave rise to much that he decried in his preaching. His lifting of the requirement of "visible sainthood," the recitation of saving faith for church membership, probably did much to encourage men to be content with mere morality and a "historical faith." This was, after all, all that was required now for membership. He relied

12. Preached and published in Boston in 1700.

heavily on the ceremony of covenant renewal to stem the tide of declining piety.[13] But this communal, liturgical act by which whole congregations and even commonwealths renewed their covenant with God was a purely external function. It consisted in reaffirming vows of purity of life and belief in Christianity. It too probably led men to feel that they could "get right with God" by a series of purely external and volitional actions. Willard's emphasis in covenant renewal was always on man's responsibility and his will.[14] The irony of Willard's ministry is that as an antidote to the declension he could only recommend the same emphasis on duty and will that he knew was the cause of it. He could diagnose a problem for which he could find no remedy.

And so at the turn of the century he issued a warning that is uncanny in its prediction of controversy to come.

> Hence what caution had Gospel ministers in their preaching up of moral duties. . . . If they preach them as to revive the Covenant of Works, to advance the Righteousness of man, and to depreciate the righteousness of Christ, they are far from being the Ministers of Christ. . . . Nor indeed do I know of anything which doth more threaten the understanding of true Christianity, and the bringing in of another Gospel, than the putting of Moral Virtues into legal dress, and without any more ado, to commend them to us as the Graces of our Christian religion. [*MNR*, pp. 96–97]

At the time of this warning, the next generation of local preachers with names such as Chauncy, Mayhew, and Briant was yet unborn. Yet Willard's warning was one that would never be heeded in Boston.

13. See *Covenant Keeping, The Duty of a People, The Necessity of Sincerity in Renewing Covenant.*

14. See *Duty of a People.*

4

Cotton Mather (1663–1728)

For some the name of Cotton Mather [1] is almost synonymous with American Puritanism itself. The third-generation Puritan clergyman, grandson of the patriarchs John Cotton and Richard Mather, seemed almost destined by geneology to be a Puritan divine. His father, Increase Mather, was one of the most influential men of his day in both church and state. Cotton Mather seems to have inherited his father's drive to mesh ecclesiastical and political influence. Born in 1662 and educated at Harvard, he was at age twelve the youngest student to have been admitted there. His first inclination was toward science, and he studied medicine until he turned to theology and became his father's assistant. In his approach to nature and the rise of witchcraft and in his support of the new technique of inoculation, he continued his early "empirical" interest in the observation and recording of data. As an outspoken opponent of Andros he was a popular figure. This popularity declined somewhat with the controversies over the witchcraft trials, the new charter, and the control of Harvard College, in which he and his father were deeply involved. He died in 1728, less than ten years before the "surprising conversions" would break out along the western edge of the colony. Whether Cotton Mather would have supported the awakening or not can only be conjectured.

One can already see from our story that Cotton Mather

1. The biographical material for this section comes from *DAB* and Perry Miller, *The New England Mind: From Colony to Province* (Boston: Beacon, 1966). I have also had access to an excellent unpublished dissertation, "Cotton Mather and the Catholic Spirit," by Joyce Ransome (University of California at Berkeley).

lived at a time of rapid change in the theological, as well as the ecclesiastical and political, condition of New England. Often regarded as a reactionary, in truth he was as much a harbinger of the new order as a guardian of the old one. Much of his life and times, the controversies in which he seemed constantly engaged, and his influence on American history have been discussed in other studies. We will concentrate on the aspect of his life relevant for our purposes—his place in the developing trends of American Puritanism at the turn of the century. Cotton Mather was as strict a believer in divine sovereignty as was Willard, but he inclined himself and those whom he influenced in the direction that Willard condemned as "moralism."

For Cotton Mather, God's sovereignty was the sovereignty of a creator. The absolute character of God's sovereignty is derived from the fact that he created everything and therefore is the Lord over it.

> The Great God who formed all things, has an absolute Dominion over all his works, to do even what he pleases with them all and it becomes His creatures humbly to Tremble, with all possible Resignation before His Holy Sovereignty.[2]

The relationship of the world to God, and particularly of man to God, is that of creature to creator, of works to their maker. All Cotton Mather's theology is derived from this basic perception of the universe as a "work" of God and of God as supreme volition, the primary agent.

The idea of God as an agent fit nicely with certain trends in the intellectual climate of early eighteenth-century America. The one place where it rubbed was the doctrine of predestination. Many men of the eighteenth century rejoiced to assert God's volitional sovereignty over nature, but many balked at

2. *The Way of Truth Laid Out,* p. 50. Hereafter cited in the text of this chapter as *WT.*

asserting it over man. Cotton Mather was not one of them. Although he acknowledged that the doctrine of predestination was coming under heavy attack in his day and that some suggested it should not be mentioned from the pulpit,[3] he was never one to duck an issue. Rather, taking his cue from the Thirty-nine Articles of the Anglican church,[4] he affirmed the most rigorous possible doctrine of predestination (pp. 2–4). The irony of this was probably not lost on his hearers, because the Anglican church was a symbol of liberalism and latitudinarianism in his day.

The need to attack Arminianism was deeply ingrained in the marrow of New England divines. From the founding fathers to the eighteenth century, the spiritual descendants of Arminius were considered, along with antinomians, the principal enemies of truth. Cotton Mather shared in this almost hereditary need to do battle with the supporters of "free-will." He chose to do so in the terms on which the battle would be fought, and finally lost, in Boston in the course of the eighteenth century. The ammunition he chose against the Arminians was the doctrine of predestination, which he stated in its strongest terms.

> The Most High God, from all eternity does most Exactly foreknow and his infallible foreknowledge does imply His eternal decree to determine it; who shall and who shall not, be brought unto the enjoyment of Him in Everlasting Blessedness. [*WT,* p. 51]

Mather continued, as his ancestors had, to weld together in the tightest bond the doctrine of predestination and the rejection of Arminianism, although some had suggested that belief in free will was not necessarily a rejection of the divine sovereignty. And so it would come to pass that those who wanted to maintain man's free will began with an attack on the doc-

---

3. *Free Grace Maintained and Improved,* p. 2. Unless otherwise identified, subsequent citations in the text of this chapter are to this work.

4. Article Seventeen defends a rigorous doctrine of predestination.

trine of predestination. And those who would defend the divine sovereignty must reject the "modern, prevailing notion of that freedom of the will." The stage for the later eighteenth-century controversies was set. Gone were the attempts of men such as Perkins, Norton, and Willard to reconcile the divine and human agencies.

Some Arminians tried to separate God's foreknowledge from his foreordination. God elected those who he foresaw would, by their own free will, enter into salvation. Cotton Mather saw through this subterfuge. The elect, he said, are chosen before time began. A "Ridiculous Absurdity" he called it, "to imagine, that man is not Elected, until God has waited all the time of a man's life, to see whether he will Persevere in a course of Well-doing" (p. 13).

Other Arminians suggested that since Christ died "for all men," grace would be available to all to save them. Mather rejects the idea that Christ died for all men in the sense of every person; rather, like Willard, he subordinates Christ's work to the doctrine of election. Thus Christ died only for the elect (pp. 17–18).

> The Arminian Universal Redemption we reject with just abhorrence. The Satisfaction of our Lord Redeemer, was not intended by Him, for the Redemption of all mankind; nor was it intended any further than His intercession is, which reaches only to the Elect of God.[5]

The position Cotton Mather rejected is the one Chauncy would try so surreptitiously to introduce into Boston society.

Mather would not live to see outright universalism advocated in the Puritan citadel of New England, but he saw the issue coming in the growing tendency toward Arminianism, and he tried to block it with the doctrine of predestination (p. 6). History would show that the doctrine of predestination was not a very effective barricade against the new age of humanism.

5. *The Resolved Christian*, p. 9.

We have traced, to some extent, the complicated relationship between the absolute nature of election and the conditional nature of the covenant, as it was worked out by several
American Puritans. It is interesting that Cotton Mather would
have little to do with any of this, perhaps as a result of his
intense attack on Arminianism. He rejected any idea that the
new covenant has conditions required of man (p. 16). "Our
Election is indeed Absolute. No Decree of God is conditional,
tho God may decree a Condition. It were derogating to the
Perfection of God, for his decree to depend upon any Condition" (p. 12). Conditional covenants, he said, play into the
hands of the Arminians by making salvation contingent upon
man's will so that God can foreknow but cannot foreordain (p.
16). The rejection of conditional covenants flowed from his
refusal to separate foreknowledge from predestination.

For Cotton Mather, the doctrine of election precluded any
idea of a conditional covenant of redemption.

> It is not left unto the meer Will of Man, to determine
> who shall by Repenting and Believing, arrive to the Bene-
> fits purchased by our Lord Redeemer. But a will to Re-
> pent and Believe is the gift of God . . . and if the Will
> to look after Salvation be bestowed only on the elect . . .
> it follows that Salvation itself runs parallel with election.
> [*WT*, p. 52]

Not only did Cotton Mather deny man any natural ability or
redemption any contractural character in the name of election
but also he seemed to return to the tradition of his grandfather, John Cotton. He appeared to convert the divine sovereignty into a demand for the kind of total humiliation to
which Firmin objected.

> When an Unregenerate man has employ'd his Natural
> Abilities towards his own Regeneration, is the Great God
> obliged now to bestow His Grace upon him? When an
> ungodly man has gone as far as Meer Nature can carry

him, he must humbly acknowledge that the most high God may still justly with-hold Special and Saving grace from him. He must lye at the foot of the Divine Sovereignty, confessing that Free Grace does all. . . . [*WT*, p. 58]

We have also traced the way in which some clergymen expressed the divine sovereignty in terms of a means–ends argument. God ordains not only the end of salvation but also the means by which that end is achieved. Faith and repentance may not be conditions of redemption but they are the means to it. Cotton Mather, following in the footsteps of his teachers, emphasized that man can only be saved through the means to redemption (p. 37). Men are elected not only to salvation but also to the means of faith and repentance.

Election and reprobation are functions of the divine sovereignty and therefore are hidden within the deep recesses of the divine plan. No man has access to this divine counsel; so no man can judge whether he is a reprobate (pp. 34–35). Since a man cannot know himself to be damned, Cotton Mather insisted that he regard himself as elect (pp. 34–35). Although Christ died only for the elect, Cotton Mather assured all men that they are commanded by God to act as if they are elect and to use the means in the hope of redemption (p. 41). It is a sin, he said, to think of oneself as a reprobate (p. 34). The Gospel call is made to all; the means are put before all. Only the elect can and will respond; yet all must act as if elected and try (pp. 41, 66–70). This kind of reasoning allowed him to preach the gospel to all and even to command all to repent and believe and yet not deny election. For Cotton Mather, one must be a Calvinist in the study and a universalist in the pulpit.

His emphasis on sovereignty influenced his discussion of the process of conversion. No one can come to God unless God acts on him. This is due not only to the sovereignty of God's call but also to the depravity of man's fallen nature. "So Depraved is the Will of a Sinner, that He will not Repent of Sin and believe on Christ until God by a supernatural and efficacious work of Grace do not only enlighten his understanding but also change and Quicken and Renew his Will" (*WT*, p. 56). This combination of divine sovereignty and human depravity led Cotton Mather to reject the model of conversion found in some of his predecessors.

> There is a very numerous party of men, in the World, who hold no Grace necessary to bring a sinner into a state of salvation, but only that which they call Moral Grace, or Moral Suasion; and which amounts to no more than a rational proposal of our duty, to turn from sin to God in Christ, with reasonable considerations, to excite men unto the doing of this their duty. . . . All they will allow Grace to do is to propose unto the Will, and leave the Will Indifferent. . . . In the mean time, they ascribe such a Vast Power unto the Will of sinful Man, that they expressly assert, the Will of man cannot be determined unto its acts by an irresistible motion . . . no, not from the Great God Himself. [pp. 23–24]

The fact that he is addressing "a very numerous party of men" said as much about his age as this quotation does about his position.

Using the means–ends model, Cotton Mather pictured faith as the means to conversion but not the cause (*WT*, p. 54). Faith is not so much an act of man as it is a gift of the divine sovereignty. In justification, he said men must look to the righteousness of Christ and not to any act that they perform. Mather referred to his grandfather's image: faith was a passive reception of the righteousness of Christ. (*WT*, p. 67). The process of conversion involves faith and repentance, which are expressions of God's sovereign action and not of man's increased role in his conversion.

Cotton Mather's drive against the Arminians led him to play down the idea of man's freedom and emphasize rather God's determining man's will. He said that God predestines man's will "without destroying the nature, the freedom" of it, but he deprived man's will of any agency of its own. Men, he reiterated, are not "masters of their own wills" (p. 28). He was less concerned than Willard to find a way in which God can work through man's will without violating it. Rather, he said that God can utilize man's will because it is not fully self-governing (p. 30). This was especially true in the case of conversion. "Conversion is not in mans power to do or to put off" (p. 32).

Cotton Mather played down the role of man's works in conversion, but what followed was another story. Cotton Mather emphasized that justification must lead to sanctification and therefore that the works of sanctification can be a sure sign that one is saved. Justification, he said, provides "a disposition to perform good works." [6] Thus a man's true nature, his character, is revealed in what he does (*EDG*, pp. 28–30). "The actions of men are more certain indications of what is within, than all their sayings" (*EDG*, p. 32). In Cotton Mather the idea that justification entails sanctification, that men are known by their fruits, became secularized into a kind of moralism. True Christianity became synonymous with men of "good character." When this happened the rather snobbish moralism of Chauncy and Mayhew was not far away.

This kind of moralism was evident throughout Mather's preaching. To him the most important thing about the gospel was that it "has a tendency to promote what is Holy, and Just, and good." [7] This moralism was clearest when he described the golden age of primitive Christianity,[8] which he sometimes placed in the early days of the colony,[9] sometimes in the early days of Christianity (see *GOW*). Actually these times were not

6. *Essays to do Good,* p. 29. Hereafter cited in the text of this chapter as *EDG.*
7. *Reasonable Religion,* p. 17.
8. See *The Good Old Way.* Hereafter cited in the text of this chapter as *GOW.*
9. *Magnalia Christi Americana.*

too far apart in his mind, for he pictured the early church just about the same way as he did the time of his grandfathers.

What impressed him about the early Christians was not their piety or faith, but the morality of their lives. The first thing about the early church he mentioned was its "sober life." Christianity was seen as first of all a duty to moral purity (*GOW*, pp. 11 ff.); the second thing he noted was its "righteous life" (*GOW*, p. 34). "What is Christianity," he asked, "but a Law of Goodness" (*GOW*, p. 44). For Cotton Mather, primitive Christianity was sheer moralism. "This name [of Christian] Signified a Good, Kind, Helpful, Courteous, & Sweet-natured people" (*GOW*, p. 46). The third and final thing that he noted about the primitive church was its "Godly life" (*GOW*, p. 72). By this he meant that, in contrast to his own age, they were ideal Christians, who lived by strict Puritan discipline (*GOW*, p. 90).

The tendency toward moralism was probably most explicit in his *Essays to do Good,* which Benjamin Franklin is reported to have said set the course of his life.[10] They certainly do read like a slightly more pious version of *Poor Richards Almanac.* What is the Christian's duty? "An unfainting resolution to do good, and an unwearied well-doing." The *Essays* are full of hints for self-improvement. A "profitable employment of time" is most important, one must be always on the lookout for opportunities "to improve," and resolution is the key to success. What role do the Scriptures have in this plan of self-improvement. They are to be used to buttress one's resolve. "Write down your resolutions. Examin what precept and what promise you can find in the Word of God to countenance your resolutions." [11] The sovereignty of God, he said, is the assurance that the resolved Christian will succeed. It stands surety that good effort will be rewarded; it guarantees that virtue will be crowned with success.

> Those who devote themselves to good devices, and who duly observe their opportunities to do good, usually find

10. "Introductions" to the *Essays,* pp. x–xi.

11. *Essays,* pp. 13, 22, 34, 35; see also *Resolved Christian.*

a wonderful increase of their opportunities. The gracious
providence of God affords this recompense to his diligent
servants. . . . Among all the dispensations of a special
providence in the government of the world, none is less
interrupted than the accomplishment of that word "Unto
him that hath shall be given." [*EDG,* p. 36]

Religion has become simply a resource for man's own well-
being. It is a small step from here to Chauncy's gospel of self-
salvation through self-improvement. Nor is it too far to
Andrew Carnegie's *Gospel of Wealth.*

The emphasis on man as a moral creature has been combined with the necessity of good works after justification to
transform Puritan Christianity into a kind of moralism. Man
doing his duty has replaced union with Christ as the primary
homiletical category. An emphasis on man's works crept into
Cotton Mather's preaching, and the focus of his writings fell
more and more on imitating the lives of the primitive church
(cf. *GOW*). or the founders of the colony.[12] Christianity became primarily a virtuous life. For Shepard, Hooker, and
Cotton the purpose of preaching was to bring men to Christ.
Cotton Mather did not reject this evangelical emphasis; but
his own stress seemed to fall on man's duty, his responsibility
to God, family, and commonwealth.[13] At the turn of the
century, piety had been transformed into moralism.[14]

This theme was expressed in Cotton Mather's interest in the
founding of societies for the reformation of manners.[15] Religious societies were popular in German pietist circles; Mather
combined the idea of these societies with his own philosophy
of "doing good." These societies for the reformation of morals
and the encouragement of a kind of practical spirituality were
to be made up of men dedicated to promoting practical piety,
missions, and good works. The societies, voluntary in nature

12. Cf. *Magnalia.*
13. *Resolved Christian,* pp. 78 ff.
14. Cf. *Essays to do Good, The Resolved Christian, Grace Defended,
The Way to Prosperity.*
15. For a good description of these, see Ransome, "Cotton Mather."

and moralistic in emphasis, expressed Mather's tendency to reduce religion to morality.

The same emphasis on duty and will undergirded Cotton Mather's reliance on the ceremony of covenant renewal. Samuel Willard shared the hope that men could be reformed and piety rekindled by getting people to "renew" the covenant. Mather emphasized that baptized people have a special claim on God and therefore a special responsibility to renew the covenant. Children baptized as infants have "special and stronger bonds upon them, to Renew the Dedication when they come to know of it" (*WT*, p. 81). This was not based on the sacramental theory of baptism that we noted in Firmin. Rather, like Willard, Mather said that baptism seals the children into the covenant (*WT*, pp. 83–84).[16] This obviously carried a certain homiletical weight with the offspring of the halfway covenant. The fact that the children of the halfway covenant had a special responsibility to God gave the ministers a certain authority over them even though they were not full members.

Cotton Mather's sermon *The Midnight Cry* was an evangelical oration, but the exhortation did not call upon men to join with Christ but rather to renew their covenant. Mather's evangelism was not directed primarily to the unchurched but to those already partially committed to the church. The covenant renewal that he advocated was a purely external and basically moralistic process directed toward avoiding a long list of offenses.[17] The pledge to do one's duty and to try to live more soberly was all that seemed required to renew the covenant. Like Willard, Cotton Mather saw the renewal of the covenant as an instrument to rekindle piety and as the preacher's only weapon against the declension.

This created the same irony in Cotton Mather's preaching that it did in Willard's. Constantly lamenting the decline of inward piety, Cotton Mather can only recommend external

16. For Willard, see *The Duty of a People that have Renewed their Covenant with God*.

17. *The Midnight Cry*, pp. 64–65, pp. 67–71.

remedies for it. Forced by the unique status of the numerous halfway members to emphasize man's duty more and more, he came close to that kind of "legal" preaching that he condemned. In making religion the resource for the age's search for self-improvement, he practically reduced religion to morality. It was this equation of religion with morality that finally triumphed over the orthodoxy Mather tried so hard to defend.

Cotton Mather, then, was almost a mirror image of the turn of the century. In his emphasis on divine predestination and man's inability, he is a child of the seventeenth century. In his tendency toward moralism and the reduction of Christianity to duty, he is a harbinger of things to come. This is also true of his approach to nature. As the century turned, men turned with a new interest toward nature, where they found, as we shall see from men like Colman and Gay, an orderliness and purposefulness that caught their imagination. The new philosophy of Newton was in the air. In 1683 Cotton's father, Increase Mather, had founded a society to discuss issues relating to the new science. In 1713 Cotton was elected a fellow of the Royal Society.

Cotton Mather was so enthralled by what he found in nature that he came perilously close to putting nature on a par with Scripture as a source of knowledge about God.

> Chrysostom, I remember, mentions a two-fold book of God; the book of the creatures and the book of the Scriptures. . . . We will now read the former of these books, it will help us in reading the latter; they will admirably assist one another. . . . All men are accomodated with that public library [the book of nature]. Reader, walk with me into it, and see what we shall find so legible there, "that he that runs may read it." [18]

The extent to which Calvin felt that man could know God through nature is a matter of dispute.[19] But it is clear that he

18. *The Christian Philosopher,* p. 11. Hereafter cited in the text of this chapter as *CP.*

19. This point is discussed in the *Institutes of the Christian Religion,* Book One (Philadelphia: The Westminster Press, 1960).

felt that because of the fall, no significant knowledge of God could come from nature. The Scriptures were necessary both to give accurate knowledge of God and to interpret the light of nature. American Puritans such as Shepard deviated from Calvin a little. Shepard clearly says that fallen man can know of God's existence and some of his attributes through nature.[20] Since saving knowledge came only from Scripture, the early Puritans were not very interested in natural knowledge of God. Cotton Mather clearly was, and he went so far as to suggest that nature can help in reading Scripture (the exact opposite of Calvin's position). And the idea of a common, public knowledge of God, available to all men through nature, was the basis of the deist attack on orthodoxy that was already beginning in England.

What Cotton Mather saw in nature is indicative of his basic attitudes. Benjamin Colman and Lemuel Briant saw in nature the model of the divine glory and purposefulness and the images of order and precision. Cotton Mather found in nature opportunities to learn the lessons of morality and duty. His *Christian Philosopher* attempted to teach his brand of pious moralism from the textbook of nature. Hail, he said, should call to mind the duty of repentance (*CP*, pp. 67–68). Thunder and lightning should call a man to meditate of his mortality (*CP*, pp. 70–71). Air reveals to man the blessings of God and the duty of thanksgiving and praise (*CP*, pp. 74–75). Wind indicates the mercy of God. "What ever point of the compass the wind blows upon, it may blow some good thoughts into our minds" (*CP*, p. 78). Cold should remind man of the wrath of God. Gravity should set one thinking on the constant and universal providence of God. (*CP*, pp. 80, 92–95). And the sea should remind one of the contrast between the bountiful goodness of God and the troubles of this world (*CP*, p. 102). Cotton Mather found the maxims of practical piety written in the book of nature. The natural law provided a foundation

20. *The Sincere Convert,* chap. 1, in *The Works of Thomas Shepard,* vol. 1.

for the instructions in self-improvement contained in his *Essays to Do Good*.[21]

But the approaching Age of Reason could not be tamed simply by converting the book of nature into a textbook for Christian moralism. Cotton's father had studied and traveled in England, as had his adversary Benjamin Colman. Cotton Mather was no doubt aware of the trends in English thought indicated by the names of Toland, Tyndall, Chillingsworth, and Locke. It says something about the age in which he lived that he had to write two attacks on the Socinians (*WT*, pp. 39 ff).[22] Firmin's fears were coming true. Even in America, in 1713, Cotton Mather had to directly confront those who wanted too much reason mixed in with their religion.

> Many hearers do much admire that which they call Rational Preaching; but when they have oppos'd it unto Scriptural Preaching, they have but betray'd a sufficient want of Reason. The most shallow Divines, and the most empty Harangues, have most unjustly been sometimes distinguish'd by the Name of Rational. Whereas, the more Gospel there is on our preaching, the more reason there is in it.[23]

Cotton Mather died long before the full impact of the Age of Reason on his country, but the subtler trends toward rationalism and Arminianism were already under way in New England when he died in 1728. It is only a matter of speculation which side he would have taken in the controversy between the supporters of the awakening, with their emphasis on sovereignty and election, and the opposers of the awakening, with their interest in morality and duty. He is one of the last people we will consider who held together in some balance the two streams in American Puritanism, one of which would be tapped by the Arminians and the other of which would be tapped by the revivalists.

21. See also *Boanerges* and *Brontologia Sacra*.

22. See also *A Christian Conversing with the Great Mystery: The Mystery of the Trinity*.

23. *Reasonable Religion*, pp. 36–37.

5

Benjamin Colman (1673–1747)

Like Cotton Mather, Colman was a mediating figure.[1] He was born in Boston in 1673 and graduated from Harvard in 1692, where he came under the tutelage of William Brattle and John Leverett, who, in the absence of President Increase Mather, were busy introducing Cartesian philosophy and Anglican latitudinarianism into the curriculum. Colman decided to supplement his education by study and travel in England. He embarked in 1695 and was captured and imprisoned by a French pirate. After this romantic adventure he finally made his way to England, where he became associated with several distinguished nonconformist clergymen, including many of liberal tendencies.

Following the Toleration Act of 1689, religious life in England was in constant controversy. The act had excluded Unitarians, yet Unitarian writings appeared in increasing numbers in England during the time Colman was there. Colman was also brought face to face with the gentle tolerance, "catholic Spirit," and charity of judgment of Anglican latitudinarians; there was also the new philosophy of Newton. As he was learning a new appreciation for nature and for man's reason, Colman became settled as a preacher in the fashionable area

1. Biographical material for this section is drawn from *DAB* and Perry Miller, *The New England Mind: From Colony to Province* (Boston: Beacon, 1966). I have looked at an unpublished dissertation entitled, "Benjamin Colman" by Charles B. Giles (University of California, Berkeley, 1963). I have used this dissertation as a source for the early part of Colman's life, but it is disappointing because it deals only with his time in England and thus gives an exaggerated picture of Colman's liberalism. There is also the dissertation "The Life and Influence of Rev. Benjamin Colman" by C. H. Chapman (Th.D., Boston University, 1947).

of Bath, England. There his sermons celebrated the excellencies of creation and of man's intellect for its ability to penetrate and describe the beauties of the cosmic machine.

Back in Boston, Increase Mather had returned from England to take charge of the college once more. He was not happy with the turn of events under Leverett and Brattle, who were not only liberalizing the curriculum but also were advocating that all church members, the halfway as well as the full, be allowed to attend the Lord's Supper. This was the position of Mather's sworn enemy, Solomon Stoddard. In 1699, Leverett and the Brattle brothers covenanted together to found a church on their own principles. The obvious man for the job as pastor was Leverett's favorite pupil, Benjamin Colman. Knowing of certain opposition from Increase Mather, they advised Colman to be ordained in England and thus began the new church by violating the fundamental tenet of New England Congregationalism, that a minister can only be ordained in his own congregation.

Obviously, Colman would meet resistance from the other Boston ministers. Although Samuel Willard offered him the hand of fellowship, most of the other Boston churches refused communion with the new society. Upon arrival in Boston, Colman and the partisans of the Brattle Street Church (so-called because Thomas Brattle donated the land on a street bearing his name) drew up a manifesto stating their intentions, which began by subscribing to the Westminster Confession. Their innovations were to be ecclesiastical and liturgical, not doctrinal. Church membership was open to all of sound faith and upright life, with or without a recitation of conversion experience. All members could partake of all the sacraments. Certain changes were made in the order of service, but, although all the sponsors were infatuated with latitudinarianism and were men of catholic sentiments and charitable judgments, there is no evidence that any deviated from the prevailing Calvinist orthodoxy.

Colman lived to see the fabric of New England rent by a

controversy that paled the founding of the Brattle Street
society. Despite his love for catholic principles and his exaltation of reason, he always sided with the orthodox. It was
Colman's early interest in the revivals that prompted Edwards
to write *The Narrative of Surprising Conversions*.[2] Although
Colman condemned the emotional excesses of the revival and
illiterate lay exhorters,[3] he welcomed Whitefield as a brother
and said he was content to be a fellow worker with the grant
itinerant.[4] Having often condemned the formalism of his age,
he endorsed the revival as God's antidote to the declension.[5]
On Tuesday, 21 October 1740, the Brattle Street Church under
Colman's direction started a special Tuesday evening lecture
to be devoted to evangelistic themes in response to the awakening and Whitefield's visit.[6] Colman gave the opening sermon,
Souls Flying to Jesus Christ, pleasant and admirable to behold.
A series of Colman's evangelistic sermons was published in
Boston. After the revival was over and party lines were drawn,
he continued to side with the Calvinists. In giving his reaction
to Davenport's retractions, he still called the revival a work of
God despite Chauncy's objections.[7] He helped depose an
Arminian clergyman named Samuel Osborn from the ministry
although Osborn was supported by Chauncy and the liberals.[8]

Even though by temperament he was more like Chauncy,
in the end his position seems similar to that of his arch adversary, Cotton Mather. Although Colman might be placed
among the liberals because of his catholic principles, it must be

2. See Jonathan Edwards, *The Great Awakening*, ed. C. C. Goen (New
Haven: Yale University Press, 1972), pp. 32–46.

3. See *The Great God Magnified His Word to the Children of Men*
Hereafter cited in the text of this chapter as *GMW*.

4. *Souls Flying to Jesus Christ*, p. 7.

5. Ibid., p. 9.

6. Ibid., "Preface."

7. *A Letter from the Reverend Dr. Colman of Boston, to the Reverend
Mr. Williams* (Boston, 1744).

8. Barney Jones, "Charles Chauncy and the Great Awakening" (unpublished dissertation, Duke, 1958), pp. 256–257.

remembered that one as orthodox as Samuel Willard was a man of "enlarged" sensibilities. Cotton Mather too prided himself on being a man of catholic principles and charitable judgments, although he did not always let these principles influence his practice. Cotton Mather claimed to be the first minister in Boston to publicly advocate tolerance. Both Colman and Mather were charmed by the new beauty their Newtonian age discerned in nature. Although differing radically on ecclesiastical policies, they both made the sovereignty of God the basis of their theology. Having been offered the presidency of Harvard in 1724 and having refused, Colman spent his entire ministry at the Brattle Street Church, dying there in 1747. Like Cotton Mather, but to an even greater extent, Colman's theology was the theology of seventeenth-century orthodoxy, but his inclinations were the inclinations of the new Age of Reason.

Colman's theology is a vision of the sovereignty of God filtered through eighteenth-century cosmology. God is first of all the creator, a sovereign cause whose sovereignty is derived from his power to create and to sustain.

> God is here represented as Self-Existent and in his own time, as the blessed and only potentate, giving unto all Things their Existence and Being, visible and invisible, by an act of his Will and the Word of his Power. . . . When the worlds come into Being . . . it was meerly the sovereign will of God. . . . God gave them their existence when, where, and how it pleased Him.[9]

Colman's God is still the God of absolute sovereignty: "There is no other limit to the Power of GOD but his Will." [10]

For Colman, as for his forefathers, every event is an act of the divine providence, every occurrence is ordained by God.

9. *A Brief Dissertation on the three first chapters of Genesis*, p. 5.
10. *The Credibility of the Christian Doctrine of the Resurrection*, p. 12. Hereafter cited in the text of this chapter as *CDR*.

"Every event of Providence, the dark as well as the light are
the issue and result of his infallible Foreknowledge and immutable Decrees." Although Colman praised man's reason, he
advocated a stance of humble resignation before the sovereignty of God.[11] Awareness of God's providence should yield

> resignation to the Great God in all His Unsearchable
> Providence: Whether of a Personal and Private Reference
> or of a Public Nature and Concern. However God dis-
> poses of us or our families or what ever He orders con-
> cerning Nations and Kingdoms of the earth, or how dark
> soever His Providence may look with respect to His
> Church, His cause and Interest thro' the World; we must
> be still and know that He is God, who will be exalted in
> the earth. The Highest Creatures owe an Absolute sub-
> mission to the Will of the Unsearchable God.[12]

Rather than going along with the liberal preachers in England
and America in playing down the theme of divine sovereignty
in favor of man's own autonomy and self-assertiveness, Colman
chose to emphasize God's sovereignty and the need for even
"the highest creatures" to submit themselves to it. "We in
solemn manner Adore the Soverain God in his Dispensations
and Abase ourselves before Him in profound Humiliation." [13]
   If Colman agreed with former generations in claiming for
God absolute sovereignty and for man complete humiliation,
he used the theme of divine sovereignty in a new way. The
Puritan God of sovereignty, we have noted, is a God who acts,
who works, who is best characterized under the rubric of divine
decrees as purposeful will. In the eighteenth century, men
excited by Newton found in nature a new orderliness that was
contingent and purposeful. Such categories as contingency,
order, and purposefulness are images of will. It was easy to see

11. *The Vanity of Man as Mortal*, pp. 28–30.
12. *A Humble Discourse on the Incomprehensibleness of God*, p. 72.
Hereafter cited in the text of this chapter as *HD*.
13. *A Brief Enquiry*, p. 9.

the new-found order in nature as the expression of the divine will. Thus the Puritan idea of God as sovereign volition fit in nicely with the eighteenth-century cosmology.

God then was one who works. Colman went further than his predecessors, and further than Cotton Mather, in deducing from this fact that God could be known from his works like any other agent. The combination of the Puritan theme of divine sovereignty and the Newtonian theme of natural order gave Colman a new emphasis on God's works and particularly the work of creation.[14] God, he said, is clearly manifest in his works, of which there are three: creation, providence, and redemption (*HD*, p. 26). And much of his emphasis falls upon the first.

> Your Bibles my dear Hearers, and the Spirit of God within you, you children of the Most High; direct and teach you to be daily reading through the vast Roll of Nature, written within and without, the Glories of the Divine Majesty. [*GG*, p. 17]

God's works then are as much a source of knowledge about him as are the Scriptures.

This does not mean that Colman put the knowledge of God through his works on a par with God's revelation. He did not go the way of the deists and suggest that nature provides a clearer knowledge of God than does revelation.

> In a Magnificent Manner God has made his name, Himself, known to us. In the Works of Creation and Providence; but most of all in his Word: The Wonders of grace exceed those of Nature; the Discoveries by Revelation are much greater than those by Reason. [*GMW*, p. 7]

God's revelation of himself in nature is indirect, mediated by his works; his revelation in Scripture is more direct. "The

14. Cf. *Humble Discourse, The Glory of God in the Firmament of his Power* (hereafter cited in the text of this chapter as *GG*), *The Lord Shall Rejoice in his Works*.

Word of God is magnificent in itself. As GOD is excellent, so must his Word be. It is the Image and Picture of his Divine Majesty, drawn by his own Pencil" (*GMW*, p. 7). Scripture exceeded nature as a source of revelation because Scripture reveals Christ and man's redemption. The knowledge of God as redeemer was far superior to the general knowledge about God gained from nature (*GMW*, pp. 11, 21, 23, 24).

When Colman turned to nature directly, he mirrored the Newtonian wonder at the cosmic machine.

> What mighty bodies are these, and how mighty motions? for Swiftness, constancy, Order and Use! And how powerful the Gravitation, Attraction, magnatism, or what shall we call their unknown mutual influence on each other. . . . Thus with utmost Ease by the wisdom and power of God, each heavenly body performs its great motion: and without such a principle (given by God) our new philosophy teaches us that Motion had never been and would soon perish. [*GG*, p. 10]

Colman, like Cotton Mather, saw in each aspect of nature a theological analogue. "O the power and goodness of God to us in that air we breathe in! It is the firmament of his power about us which holds our souls in Life." The glory of God, he said, is shown in the "elasticity of air . . . which insensibly yields to bodies in their motion, yet strongly closes round them and holds them in their motion" (*GG*, pp. 7, 6).

Like many men of his time, Colman was particularly fascinated and perplexed by the problem of space, emptiness, nothingness, and vacuum. The idea of empty space was so mysterious that many, including Colman, were tempted to equate it with the mystery of God himself.[15]

> Space is so mysterious and inexplicable a thing in Nature that Men of Genius and Philosophy have been ready to deify it and say it is God himself. . . . It is the open

15. Colman refers to Isaac Watts's "First Philosophical Essay" on God as Space in *Glory of God*, pp. 16–17.

Volume of nature, in which we should early begin to read the Name of God, and read on in it as long as we live, and more and more adore Him in his Incomprehensibleness. [*GG*, p. 16]

In the end, Colman was no more able to unravel the deep mysteries of space and deity than most of his contemporaries. He took refuge from the mystery of space in the theory of "aether." "The learned cannot conceive the largest part of the creation should be perfectly void and therefore fill it with a Species of Matter under this Denomination of Aether" (*GG*, p. 4).

The natural world, he said, suffers as a result of man's fall and thus clearly does not reveal God. The cursing of the ground in Genesis meant that the world bears the marks of man's sin (*GMW*, p. 20) and therefore offers a distorted picture of God. Nature as God's work does mirror God, as do his works of providence and redemption, but there is no real natural theology in Colman. God's existence and attributes are reflected in the cosmic order, but they are not proven thereby. Because of the fall, not all men can read the book of nature but only those who have been illuminated by God's revelation in Scripture (*GG*, pp. 2–3).

Besides undermining the efficacy of revelation in nature, Colman also gave it a distinctly Christian cast. The purpose of God's glory in nature is to draw men to Christ (*GG*, pp. 15–21). Since true revelation is only contained in God's Word, both the Christ and the Scriptures, whatever revelation there may be in nature must be related to them. Not universal knowledge of God but particular knowledge of Jesus Christ was the goal of Colman's discourses on nature. "The firmament is the Book and School of Jesus Christ, and he sends us to it to learn respecting himself" (*GG*, p. 17). Thus Colman can apply the images drawn from nature not only to God but also to Christ, his Church, and the Scriptures (*GG*, pp. 17–21).

We must leave this eighteenth-cetury combination of science

and piety. In discussing nature, Colman's favorite form of punctuation was the exclamation mark. The awe and wonder he felt before nature was synonymous with his awe and wonder before God. He did not try to prove God from nature or deduce the character of God from the order of the cosmos as much as he took nature as a model for understanding God. The vastness and incomprehensibility of nature were images for the vastness and incomprehensibility of God, just as the mystery of space was an analogue to the mystery of the God-head (*HD,* pp. 25–49; see also *GG*). According to Colman, man has no immediate knowledge of God himself during this life. All revealed knowledge, whether by works or word, is in-direct, relying on images rather than on a direct perception of God. It is only a shadow of God's real self.

> We that have no Immediate Vision of His Glory, but see as thro' a Glass darkley; thro' the glass of his Works, His Word, and Ordinances. A glass gives but a weak and lan-guid Representation, a vanishing and transient Glimpse. We rather can say what God is not, than what He is. [*HD,* p. 6]

What nature really reveals then is "the Immensity, Omni-presence, and Incomprehensibleness of God" (*CDR,* p. 14; see also *HD, GG*). The mystery of nature is one with the mystery of God. Colman used nature to emphasize the stan-dard Puritan themes of the sovereignty, glory, and transcen-dence that he calls the "incomprehensibleness" of God. This emphasis on the mysterious and unsearchable character of God made him virtually unknowable and far beyond man's ken (*CDR,* p. 38). God is a God of will, standing mysteriously behind and beyond his works and revealed only indirectly by them. Thus a kind of agnosticism results under the guise of reverence. Colman was as driven as any of his forebears to give all glory to God, but by equating his glory with his incom-prehensibleness, he made God himself practically unknow-able. The mystery of God shifted the focus of theology from

God himself (which is unknowable) to his works (which can be known).

Unlike the deists, Colman did not limit God's works to creation. God not only created the world, he also providentially cares for it and redeemed it when it fell under the bondage of sin. The strong emphasis on God's will that we observed in reference to creation continued in the discussion of redemption. For Colman the doctrine of election was central since God's will was a primary theological category (*CDR*, p. 10).[16] God's electing will was one with his redeeming will because he wills to call some men to share in redemption.

Colman understood the atonement in terms similar to those noted throughout this study. Man sinned and transgressed the law, and God's justice demanded punishment. God's law must not be invalidated in the process of forgiving man, so Christ comes as a sacrifice. He obeys the law and bears the punishment, saving man, who could not save himself. Thus Colman, refusing to see Christ primarily as a teacher, continued to emphasize man's inability and the necessity of Christ's sacrifice. A strong emphasis on substitutionary atonement persisted in Colman (*CDR*, pp. 19–20; *GMW*, pp. 16–20).[17] Even in his sermons on nature, Colman always returned to man's need for redemption in Christ.[18]

What is man's role in this universe ruled by the sovereign will of God? We noted before that an increased attention to man's reason went along with the emphasis on nature. It is man's reason, after all, that discovered the beauties of the cosmic harmony.

> MAN, MAN, He is the Creature here below, form'd for giving Praise to God. Man's Mind and eye and ear, his mouth and Breath, his Tongue and Lips; his hands and

16. *Lord Shall Rejoice*, p. 16.
17. *The Unspeakable Gift of God: A Right and Beautiful Spirit*, pp. 17–18; *Souls Flying*, pp. 20–21.
18. See *Glory of God; Humble Enquiry*.

knee are made for Worship and Adoration, Praise and Thanksgiving, his eye sees thro' the Universe, his mind should contemplate every Divine Perfection in all he sees. [*GG,* p. 13]

Colman reminded his congregation that God delights in man,[19] whose physical as well as spiritual nature is a wonder to behold. "Among all the rich variety of living creatures upon the earth . . . there is none to be compared with the Body of man for beauty and elegance" (*CDR,* p. 17).

This exaltation of man was set in the context of a doctrine of the atonement that emphasized man's inability. Colman was clear that the glorious aspects of man's life were lost by the fall.[20] Since the fall, "our nature is corrupted, our Souls enfeebled and disabled, indisposed and adverse to what is holy and good. Our moral and spiritual powers are gone from us and as it were wither'd away." [21] Even man's reason, which for Colman formed man's very essence, was of no use in his salvation.

Look we into the Ages and Places of this World that have been left to bare Discoveries of Reason, and it is easie to observe of all their searchings after God, and that they felt and grop'd as in the Dark. . . . The World by wisdom knew not God. Mans lusts soon put out the light of Reason, and the light that was in them became darkness.[22]

Despite man's power to conquer the universe, he remained in the place where Calvinists have always seen him, fallen and unable to contribute to his own salvation.

Colman, like his contemporaries and immediate predecessors, defined man as a moral agent. Man is a living Soul, not only in respect to Immortality, but also because "he is an intelligent, self-conscious, creature, made a law to Himself, and

19. *Lord Shall Rejoice,* p. 11.
20. *Vanity of Man,* pp. 18–21.
21. *The Wither'd Hand Stretched Forth,* p. 5.
22. *Brief Enquiry,* p. 4.

for self government, an agent by counsel, accountable to God, to his own conscience, and to the societies to which he belongs." [23] God works on man as such in the process of conversion by means of commands that appeal to his moral agency and responsibility.[24]

What of man's inability? Colman said that at the same time that God gives the command, he supplies man with the grace to overcome his natural inability. "It is in no way unjust or absurd for God to command us to do those things which of ourselves we are unable to do because He is able to make all grace abound to us and give us an alsufficiency in all things." [25] Thus, although theology instructs man in his inability, man cannot plead that as an excuse before God. Whatever theoretical inability theology gives to man, God more than makes up for it by supplying him with a practical ability that he can use.

> Wilt thou know O Vain man that there is something you have to do which God requires and expects, & which he will make you to do if ever his mercy and grace do take effect upon you. You have natural powers made for use and you can't pretend that you cannot think, consider of things and reason with yourself about them, and wish and ask of God his Pity, Help, and Pardon, his Influence and Power upon thy poor languid Soul. Altho' your strength and limbs are utterly gone, yet you can ly and look up unto God on high to perform all things for you . . . only look to Jesus and He can give thee faith to be healed . . . come, ly not still at Christ's call and say not unto Him, I cannot stir! It were a reproach to his calling thee, and to suspect his Power or Truth! For will He require of thee that which he will not help thee to do? For tho' of thy self thou canst do nothing to a saving effect upon thy

23. *Brief Dissertation,* p. 12.
24. *Wither'd Hand,* pp. 15–19.
25. Ibid., p. 16.

soul, yet Christ strengthening thee thou shalt be able to do all things, whatsoever he says unto thee. Thou art not a Stock neither in respect of motion nor a meer brute creature in respect of understanding.[26]

The above passage is probably totally contradictory, but it is not so much a contradiction in Colman's thought as in his culture. Trying to preserve both the old emphasis on man's inability and the new humanism of the age was, during Colman's lifetime, becoming a contradiction too heavy to bear intellectually and psychological. Among his colleagues were those who had to let go of the idea of man's inability in order to preserve the spirit of the times and those that set themselves wholly against the age in order to preserve the old teaching.

Colman did not help the problem of the will by stating it in terms of two contradictory causes, man and God. Rather than the harmony between them that Willard and Norton tried to create, Colman and Cotton Mather saw the issue in terms of one cause overturning the other. Colman's constant emphasis was on God making man do what man wills in his conversion. In the end Colman could only say that in redemption man's actions are "by no means done at last without the Will of God over-ruling them" (*HD*, p. 70).

Colman tempered the humanism of the new age in the direction of traditional Puritanism by reiterating that man was made to glorify God.[27] Man is not an end in himself; rather he is to "serve, worship, obey, honour and glorify God . . . and to enjoy him forever" (*CDR*, p. 18). Man is always subsumed under God. The attributes of man in which Colman took pleasure are those that enable man to worship and praise God. Colman's exaltation of man is an exaltation of man's ability to serve God and not himself.

Colman's life and writings therefore exemplify all the forces at work on the eve of the awakening. The Brattle Street

26. Ibid., p. 14.
27. *Brief Dissertation*, pp. 13, 15–16.

Church was a symbol of the liberalism of the new age, but its pastor endorsed the great revival with its attempts to reassert the theology of the old age in the teeth of the dawning of the new one. Colman turned the focus of theology on nature in a new way, but he found there the traditional themes of God's sovereignty and providence. He delighted in man with a new relish, but it was man's ability to give glory to God that most excited him. Neither the humanism nor the theocentrism, neither the emphasis on reason nor the exaltation of revelation would disappear in the history of American religion. The battle between them continues to the present day. What would be lost after the clash of these seemingly contradictory forces at the time of the awakening would be the drive for synthesis and balance that characterized the beginning of New England Puritanism. The crisis of the Great Awakening marked the end of Puritanism not only because of the innovations of both the Arminians and the revivalists, but also because of the loss of the balance and synthesis that continued in Colman and puts him on the boundary between the seventeenth and the eighteenth centuries.

6

Solomon Stoddard (1643–1729)

Commanding respect by the sheer weight of his presence as he surveyed the colony from the high pulpit in Northampton, Massachusetts, Solomon Stoddard set himself resolutely against the trends of his time.[1] Best known for the ecclesiastical revolution that historians named after him, in truth his rejection of the polity and practice of the Boston churches was just one episode in a continuing battle with his age and with everything that Boston would come to represent politically and theologically in the course of the eighteenth century.

New England social theory, with its stratification of mankind into fixed classes, held that some men were born aristocrats and rulers; Solomon Stoddard was an archetype of this superior class of men. Stoddard's father, Anthony, was a prosperous merchant when he arrived with the founding fathers. He married Mary Downing, a niece of Governor Winthrop and a sister to Sir George, after whom Downing Street was named. Anthony Stoddard's wealth and family increased at the same rate. Mary bore him fifteen children, including Solomon, who was born in 1643. Solomon Stoddard graduated from Harvard in 1662, taking as his commencement thesis the proposition that "God punishes sin by a necessity of nature." However common that thesis may have been in 1662, by the turn of the century such a stark affirmation of God's abhorrence of sin and sinners could be taken as an attack on the

---

1. Biographical information for this section is drawn from *DAB* and Perry Miller, *The New England Mind: From Colony to Province* (Boston: Beacon, 1966), and his article, "Solomon Stoddard," *The Harvard Theological Review* (1941): 277–320, in which can be found the sources for the quotations used in the biographical section.

foundations of the new age symbolized by Chauncy's sermon entitled "The benevolence of the deity."

After graduation Stoddard became the first librarian of the college. For reasons of health, he had to spend the years 1667–1669 in Barbados as chaplain to the Independents. Arriving back in Boston, he was ready to sail to England, despite its inhospitable climate for Independents after the Restoration. Before he could leave he was invited to preach at Northampton. Eleazar Mather, the first pastor at Northampton and brother of Increase, had died a few months earlier, leaving a widow, three children, and an empty pulpit and parsonage. Solomon Stoddard solved all these problems in one stroke. Called in March 1670, he promptly married Esther Mather and moved into his predecessor's house as well as his pulpit. Upon accepting the call, Stoddard resolved "that light and peace and the power of religion may be continued in this plantation" and to give "the residue of my dayes to the service of the house of God in this place." He spent the residue of his days, a full fifty-nine years, in that place where he brought much power but very little peace.

To Esther Mather's three children he added twelve more. Much of his eventual control over the western frontier is indicated by the interlocking lines of family and marriage that made him the trunk of a family tree whose roots and branches reached into almost every corner of the Connecticut valley. Their second child, named for her mother, married the Reverend Timothy Edwards of Windsor, Connecticut, and had, in Stoddard fashion, ten daughters and one son named Jonathan. Another daughter married the Reverend William Williams of Hatfield; three others also married parsons, and one married the town's leading businessman, Joseph Hawley. One son, Colonel John Stoddard, was Commander-in-Chief of the Army in western Massachusetts. This geneological web, which covered the Connecticut River basin, gave Stoddard a base of power that he never failed to exploit.

His power was secular as well as ecclesiastical. He seems to

have run the town meeting and had it build a wide road from
Northampton to Boston over which he was the most regular
traveler, riding every year to Boston at commencement time to
deliver several sermons. He was the first to hear of King
Philip's conspiracy and sent several warnings to Boston that
were neglected. When war broke out in 1675, he was in the
middle of the western campaigns. In 1676 the magistrates
considered abandoning the defense of the Connecticut valley
and pulling back. Almost single-handedly Stoddard forced
them to reconsider by warning them that God's wrath would
fall upon them if they abandoned a "plantation" that he had
established. After the war Stoddard, even more firmly established in power in the valley, demanded from the colonial
government twenty pounds to recompense his personal losses
and to spare the cost to the town.

This was not the only time he confronted the colonial
capital. He was known in Boston because of his annual visits,
which clergy and laity alike are reported to have received
"with a peculiar Reverence and Pleasure." He publicly blamed
the affliction of King Philip's War on the pride and tolerance
of Boston. Preaching the commencement sermon in 1707 he
spoke, apparently with unforgettable vehemence, against "ex-
cess in Commencem't entertainments." Then he took the
governor to Judge Sewall's house and demanded that, as a
magistrate, he suppress the sins of Boston. Fearing neither
magistrate nor minister, Stoddard never failed to speak plainly
against the positions of even the most eminent divines, as Increase and Cotton quickly learned. He was intolerant of Baptists, Indians, and the sin of man. By his power he had the
General Court pass a series of laws against overluxurious wearing apparel and had twenty-three persons in Northampton
fined in one session for "wearing silk in a flaunting manner
and for long hair and other extravagences contrary to honest
and sober order." He touched everything with an iron hand;
in Northampton his hegemony earned him the nickname
"Pope." Timothy Dwight, who learned from his grandfather
(who was Stoddard's grandson) the intricacies of the Con-

necticut valley, said Stoddard "possessed, probably, more influence than any other Clergyman in the province."

Upon arrival in Northampton, Stoddard accepted the halfway covenant that his predecessor had violently opposed. Sometime before 1677 he quietly but firmly introduced the practice called Stoddardism, which allowed all baptized persons full membership. He advocated this practice in the teeth of Increase and Cotton Mather during the synod of 1679. His power was great enough that he brought most of the churches in western Massachusetts and the Connecticut valley along with him in his innovation. The sources of his power were his personality, his political influence, and his pulpit and preaching. In 1679, 1683, 1696, 1712, and 1718 he experienced revivals, or "harvests" as he called them, in his parish. His rejection of the halfway covenant and his homiletical vehemence were directed at the same end—to produce conversions.

By 1725 Stoddard had never missed a Sunday service or weekday lecture due to illness for fifty-five years, nor would he miss one for the next four. But the town voted in April that it was time to find an assistant for their aging pastor. Perhaps as a tribute to Stoddard they called one of his own family, his grandson Jonathan Edwards, who settled in 1726. In February 1729, Stoddard died. Funeral sermons were preached up and down the valley and in Boston. His son-in-law William Williams preached the oration in Northampton, praying that the prophet's mantle would fall upon Stoddard's successor, who was also William's nephew. The spirit fell with so much power that the town could not cope with him, and so twenty years later the same Williams family and other close kin drove Edwards from Northampton. Despite his break with Stoddard's policy on the sacraments (which was the final straw for the town of Northampton), behind all Edwards's attacks on Arminianism, the rise and growth of which he have traced in this study, stood the spirit of Solomon Stoddard.

The difference between Stoddard and the rest of the ministers of the colony did not arise from the distance, either in-

tellectual or geographical, between the frontier town of Northampton and the urban center of Boston. It arose because
Stoddard began his theology from a point different from
everyone else in the brief course of American theology. For
Stoddard the basic problem of theology was not correct understanding or willing, but perceiving. For Stoddard, theology
did not begin with intellectual understanding or with moral
action, but rather when men saw the glory of God.

Men can perceive this glory either in God's works or in his
Word.

> When God opens the eyes of men and gives spiritual un-
> derstanding to them, there are two ways wherein they may
> see the glory of God. 1. by reasoning from the works of
> creation and common providence. . . . When they be-
> hold the work of God, they readily see, if there eyes be
> opened, that these things were made by a God of infinite
> power and wisdom, and goodness. There is a self-evidenc-
> ing light in these works of God, showing that they are
> the effects of a God of infinite glory. The world is a
> glass, reflecting the glory of God and when mens eyes are
> opened, they may plainly see it. . . . When mens eyes
> are opened, they see the force of the argument. . . . Rea-
> son enlightened by the Spirit of God teaches men con-
> vincingly what God is. 2. By reasoning from the Word of
> God. The Word of God has a self-evidencing light in it;
> it shews that it doth proceed from a God of infinite
> Glory.[2]

Stoddard used the notion, which was becoming popular at the
turn of the century, of the two books—the book of nature and
the book of the Scriptures—but in a way different from his
contemporaries. Rather than suggesting that man knows God
through nature by means of reason and through Scripture by
means of faith, he applied the Calvinist theology of the
Scripture to nature as well. Calvin said the word is "self-

2. *The Nature of Saving Conversion*, pp. 37-38. Hereafter cited in the
text of this chapter as *NSC*.

evidencing" because the Spirit that inspired the Scripture writers also inspires the Scripture readers.[3] Stoddard applied this same dialectic of Word and Spirit to nature. Nature is self-evidencing in the same way Scripture is because discerning God in nature also requires "spiritual understanding."

Unfortunately Stoddard, perhaps because he lacked access to Locke, did not carry out a sustained critique of the faculty psychology of his day, as Edwards did. Thus Stoddard was forced to describe man as a combination of faculties and so he was unable to clarify the relation between man's perceiving and his thinking and doing. Total reliance on such a faculty psychology created an unresolved confusion in Stoddard's thought between his fundamental insight that a man is what he perceives (which Edwards carried further) and his continual discussion of man in terms of what is going on in his mind or his will.

For Stoddard the most important thing about perceiving the glory of God was that it affects the will. He assumed that if men perceive the divine beauty their wills will be redirected toward God's glory and holiness.

> When men do see the glory of God, they would act against their nature if they should not be holy. . . . When men know the excellency of God, they must chuse him. The glory of God is such, that it capitulates the heart; where it is seen, it has a magnetic power; it irresistibly conquers the will; there is a necessity of loving God when he is seen. . . . There is no power in the will to resist holiness when the glory of God is seen. It is impossible in nature that men should know God and not be holy. . . . The excellency of God is a sufficient reason for men's loving and serving him. . . . The gloriousness of God has a commanding power on the heart. [*NSC*, p. 32]

The irresistible working of God has been shifted from the sovereignty of his absolute power to the irresistible nature of his aesthetic attraction. The similarity to Edwards is obvious.

3. Cf. *The Institutes of Christian Religion,* Book One, chap. 7–9.

The problem of the bondage of the will was solved by the magnetic beauty of the divine glory. The early seventeenth-century preachers had said that God must break man's bondage to sin with an overwhelming act of sovereignty. Later in the century some suggested that rational arguments could persuade men out of their bondage to sin. Stoddard agreed that men are in such captivity that only God's action can free them. But it is the irresistible attraction of God's excellency and not the forceful action of his will that turns men from sin.

> If men know God they will be holy. Where God is truly known, he will be loved and served uprightly. . . . Where once men have a spiritual sight of the glory of God, they can do no other but serve him. Light and life go together. Before men know God it is impossible that they should love him, for they are strangers to the reason and foundation of love! If they have never so many arguments set before them, to persuade, yet they cannot do it, if they strive very much with their own hearts to love God, from a fear that they shall be damned if they do not yet they cannot do it. But when their eyes are opened and they see the glory of God, they would act against their nature if they did it not.[4]

Stoddard's presupposition was the same as that of Edwards's *Treatise on the Freedom of the Will.* The will desires and naturally seeks the highest good. If it once perceives that good, it will be drawn to it like iron to a magnet. Bound up in his faculty psychology, Stoddard was never able to articulate, as Edwards did, how perception leads to willing. The best he could do was to subsume the will under the intellect [5] and then equate perception with understanding. Thus Stoddard

---

4. *Three Sermons,* pp. 71–72. Hereafter cited in the text of this chapter as *TS.*

5. "The will always follows the last dictates of the Understanding; the will itself is a blind faculty, and it follows the direction of the Understanding" (*Three Sermons,* p. 71).

concluded that when a man perceives (or "understands") the divine excellency, his will follows this understanding (*TS*, pp. 71–72, 75–76; *NSC*, p. 32). Despite his inability to explain how perceiving and willing go together, he never lost sight of the fundamental vision that they do and that the problem of theology and of conversion is actually the problem of perception. "When they see things as they are, immediately they come; that delivers them from their enmity to Christ. . . . When they see the glory of God in the face of Christ, they make no more resistance" (*TS*, pp. 75–76).

This perception of the divine glory, Stoddard said, changes man's nature by changing his "dispositions." Not only is the will irresistibly turned toward God but also it is permanently bent in that direction. "When they understand the Glory of God in the Gospel, that makes them actually turn to God and leave a disposition in the heart that way" (*TS*, p. 75). In keeping with his use of the model of sensation, Stoddard suggested that men develop a "taste" for the divine glory that they cultivate into a "habit."

> A man that has had the experience of the sweetness of honey is inclined thereby to judge so from time to time. . . . He that has understood the gloriousness of God, is prepared and disposed thereby to judge so from time to time. This discovery leaves such a sense and impression on the heart, as inclines it for ever to judge so concerning God. . . . Repeated discoveries strengthen the habit and dispose them to more readiness to judge so. [*NSC*, pp. 35–36].

Theology begins with an experience, a taste, a perception of the divine glory and excellency. When these sermons were preached in the second decade of the eighteenth century, Stoddard had already experienced three of his harvests and was probably in the midst of a fourth, and Jonathan Edwards was still a teenager in the midst of his studies at Yale.

For Stoddard this awareness of the divine glory was an

awareness of the divine sovereignty. Along with the perception of the divine beauty went a perception of the absolute dependence of all upon God.

> When the eyes of men are opened they see the gracious Nature of God, that he can have mercy on whom he will have mercy, that he can find it in his heart to have compassion on them, though they be meer creatures and uncapable of any profit to him, though they cannot recompense him . . . they see that there is an excellancy in the loving kindness of God. [*NSC*, p. 54]

Seeing the divine excellency not only turns the will toward God but also humbles it before him.

> When this Spiritual light shines into Men, and they see the gloriousness of God, they understand that all nations to him are as the drop of the bucket . . . it becomes them to be subject to his disposal in all things; to sacrifice all their interests to his glory, and to be obedient to his voice in every thing; to be abased because of their sins and lie in the dust before him. . . . When their eyes are opened to see God's glory, they see reason to lie low before him. [*NSC*, pp. 56–57]

Stoddard's perception of the world as a "glass, reflecting the glory of God" was diametrically opposed to the way of viewing the world that was developing in the eighteenth century. In men such as Gay, Briant, Chauncy, and Mayhew there was an increasing emphasis on man's moral and intellectual autonomy. Stoddard's perception was a return to the absolute dependence of man upon God as found in the early seventeenth century: but this dependence was based on the aesthetic power of God's excellency rather than the volitional power of his decrees.

This difference between Stoddard and his contemporaries was also reflected in Stoddard's use of nature. In men such as Colman and Mather, as in most theologians of the eighteenth century, nature was seen as an indirect expression of the divine will. For Stoddard, nature was the direct expression of the divine beauty. Whereas Cotton Mather used nature as a textbook in Puritan moralism and Colman used nature as a model for the divine working, Stoddard used nature as a glowing transmission of the glory of God to man. For Stoddard the purpose of this effusion of divine glory was to turn men toward God.

> If God would open the eyes of Men to see his glory in the Works of Creation, or in the Law, or in Providence, that would make men holy. There is a great deal of convincing light in these things and they discover the glory of God. [*TS*, p. 70]

Men do not learn either new intellectual concepts or new duties from nature. Rather, they experience the divine glory, and this experience rather than intellectual understanding or moral commands is what leads to holiness. "The sight of the glory of God will necessarily draw forth holy actions" (*TS*, p. 74).

It is clear from Stoddard's life and writings that his main concern was to convert men. It was not with codifying the constructions of theology as Willard did, preserving the inherited ways as Cotton Mather was motivated to do, or producing a system of Christian thought more in tune with the new age as Chauncy and Mayhew attempted to do. His principal goal was to bring men to the experience of grace, and his ecclesiological controversy with the Mathers was focused on this issue. Stoddard was more concerned with making the church and the sacraments into effective evangelical instruments than he was with preserving the past. Therefore, his theology quickly centered on the problem that had been the central concern of Puritan theologizing for the first three-quarters of the seventeenth century—the problem of conversion. Stoddard said, in the spirit of his age, "God don't deal with men as stocks and stones by meer force; but he deals with them as with reasonable creatures." "The gospel," he said, "only works in way of persuasion" (*TS,* pp. 67, 74). For Stoddard this persuasion was not one that man arrived at by his own reasoning; rather it was the irresistible result of seeing the divine glory.

Since this persuasion came through the normal faculties of perception, understanding, and will, it was not an external compulsion (*NSC,* pp. 33–34) but an irresistible action of God. God respects the integrity of man's faculties but there was no hint in Stoddard of what we have noted in others, that man is in a position to accept or refuse God's "persuasion."

This is because men are dead in sin. "They cannot deliver themselves, that it is utterly impossible for them to mend their own hearts." [6] Some of Stoddard's contemporaries suggested that although it was impossible for man to save himself on his own, he could do so with a little help from God. Stoddard would have none of that.

> He must see himself under the reigning power of sin. . . . They must see that they are under the dominion of sin, that a spirit of self-love reigns in them, and that their heart is contrary to what is good . . . their hearts are like the hearts of the devils, as full of sin as a toad is of poison. . . . He has no inclination to any thing that is good, that there is no disposition to that which is good. [*GC,* p. 68]

There is nothing in man on the basis on which he can even cooperate with God.

The key to Stoddard's idea of conversion lay in the chasm he saw between the converted and the unconverted. One is either on one side or the other, and only God's action can bring a man across into salvation. Therefore there is no possibility of any human agency in conversion. Either one is unconverted and all one's actions are worthless, or one is converted and therefore one's actions are unnecessary to obtain salvation.

6. *A Guide to Christ,* p. 69. Hereafter cited in the text of this chapter as *GC.*

There is no process in which man can participate, only a quantum jump from one state to the other.

This gulf between the two states was reflected in Stoddard's discussion of common and saving graces. They are totally different; there is no common ground between them.

> Some have been of the opinion that saving grace and common grace differ only in degree, that Sorrow for Sin increases until it becomes saving; and love to God increases till it becomes saving; But certainly, saving grace doth differ specifically from all that went before: Gracious actions are of another nature than the religious actions of natural men. [*NSC,* pp. 5–6]

In Boston, men such as Gay and Chauncy said that salvation consisted mainly in the improvement of one's natural endowments. Whereas the liberals saw a gradual ascent from nature to grace, Stoddard saw total opposition. "There is an opposition between saving Grace and common Grace. . . . Common Graces are lusts, and do oppose saving Grace: Making his own salvation his last end, is contrary to making the glory of God his last end" (*NSC,* pp. 8–9). The liberal order of salvation, first preached in Boston during Stoddard's lifetime, emphasized progressive improvement. By placing an unbridgeable gulf between the natural man and the redeemed man, Stoddard set himself against this liberal spirit.

This same chasm meant that, for Stoddard, conversion was instantaneous. For Chauncy, conversion was a process by which the natural man was gradually trained up, preferably by means of Harvard education, into the image of God. For Chauncy, conversion was like the growth of a tree from an acorn; for Stoddard it was like the explosion of a bomb.

For Stoddard faith was not a process; it was a constellation of graces, given at once. Stoddard said that faith was a condition of justification, but it almost seems as if he was making a play on words. Faith was more the condition that one is in when one is justified than it is the condition by which one is justified. He spoke of justification as conditional upon faith; but God not only sets the condition, he alone fulfills it (*TS*, pp. 76–78). Stoddard said "faith in Christ is an act of the will . . . it is a chusing of Christ for his saviour" (*GC*, p. 60). But man does not turn his own will toward Christ; rather man's will is drawn to Christ's irresistible excellency. Stoddard used the terms of his day about faith being an act of the will and redemption being conditional. But these new wineskins contained Stoddard's peculiar blend of the vintage wine of seventeenth-century Calvinism and the even newer wine that powered his grandson's vision and the Great Awakening. "Conversion is wrought by Light. God is the author of Conversion: Men must be born of the Spirit" (*NSC*, p. 28). Stoddard never lived to see the new light shine in incandescent brilliance to lighten his Connecticut valley. But even after his death, he continued to be a grandfather to men who were born of this spirit.

The eighteenth-century evangelicals' understanding of conversion (drawn from Stoddard) paralleled their understanding of the ministry; the same is true for the Arminians. For the Arminians, salvation was mainly a process of moral self-development, mostly by means of education and discipline. For them the minister was basically an instructor, a teacher, and thus they emphasized the role of education in the ministry because only an educated man could educate others. For the evangelicals, salvation was primarily an experience in the life of each man. Thus they emphasized the necessity of experience as the prerequisite for the ministry. Stoddard, who vowed to bring the power of God with him to Northampton when he accepted the call, stresseed the importance of the empirical experience of conversion. It was the drive to bring men into this experience that stood behind his view of the sacraments as "converting" ordinances, the tenor of his preaching, and consequently his view of the ministry. Ministers, he said, must

> get the Experience of this Work in their own Hearts. If they have not Experience, they will be but blind Guides,

they will be in Great Danger to entertain false Notions concerning a Work of Conversion. . . . Whatever Books men have read, there is a great need of experimental knowledge in a Minister. . . . It is a great calamity to wounded Consciences to be under the Direction of an unexperienced Minister. [*GC*, pp. 7–8]

This was said at least twenty-five years before Gilbert Tennent warned the colonies of the dangers of an unconverted ministry. Stoddard's and Tennent's statements have parallels in the writings of many of the early Puritans, particularly Perkins, Sibbes, and Preston, who were very influential in the early days of the colony as well as in Shepard, Cotton, and Hooker, who were its leading pastors.[7] As their sermons and diaries make clear, all these men were saved through the overwhelming experience of grace. They said the purpose of their preaching was the recreation of that experience in the lives of their hearers. This was particularly true after this experience was made the sine qua non of church membership. Tennent, Whitefield, and Edwards were not advocating something new in their insistence on a "converted" ministry; they were simply saying what all "experimental" divines had said. Both the evangelicals and the Arminians saw the purpose of preaching as recreating in the hearers the experiences of the preacher. For the Arminians the primary experience was education and the sermon was to educate the hearers; for the evangelicals the primary experience was conversion and the sermon sought to convert the hearers. The Arminians warned of the dangers of an uneducated ministry; the evangelicals warned of the danger of an unconverted ministry.

Stoddard's book *A Guide to Christ* was in large part a discussion of the problem of preparation. In many ways, in form as well as content, it was more like Hooker's cycle of sermons on conversion or Shepard's *Sincere Convert* than like anything being written by Stoddard's contemporaries. It is indicative of

7. See William Haller, *The Rise of Puritanism* (New York: Harper & Row, 1957).

Stoddard's thought that he went back and revived this issue, which many had thought dead for a quarter of a century. Increase Mather wrote the preface, which ended by gratuitously observing that he did not disagree with Stoddard in the "fundamentals in Religion" ("Preface" to *GC*, p. viii). It is hard to believe after the heat of the battle that Increase did not consider the nature of the church and the sacraments fundamental. He had done all in his waning power to read Stoddard out of the faith because of his position on what Increase later slightingly called "some points." Increase had earlier refused to write a preface for Stoddard's *Safety of Appearing*, and this preface was perhaps his token admission that Stoddard had won, or least fought him to a draw, and there was nothing Increase could do. As usual, Increase Mather did not understand what Stoddard was up to. His preface spoke of preparation as though it were a controversy long buried. Increase casually attempted to reconcile the writings of Hooker, Shepard, and Firmin, thus showing how far he had really come from the spirit of his revered forefathers.

Stoddard, on the other hand, understood that what was at stake in the previous controversy over preparation was still at issue in his own day. To reassert the old doctrine of preparation was to reassert the absolute sovereignty of God over the process of conversion, a sovereignty that was becoming less and less absolute in Boston as the eighteenth century wore on. Preparation, he said, keeps men from false confidence. The denial of preparation would "expose men to think themselves converted when they are not. . . . If they do not know any necessity of preparations, they will take the first appearances of Holiness for Holiness" (*GC*, p. 2). In Boston men would be told that the first signs of righteousness begin to render them redeemed; for Stoddard the idea of preparation was a safeguard against such "false hopes." The doctrine of preparation did not bolster man's confidence in his own righteousness but rather destroy it. Preparation taught men that their own first works were but common and had nothing saving in them (*GC*, p. 4).

Preparation was a safeguard against presumption in a most presumptuous age. It was not a guarantee of salvation but a purely negative doctrine that taught men not to trust their own works.

> There is no necessity in nature of any Preparation before the Infusion of GRACE. Christ changed water into wine, and raised the Dead to Life, without any previous preparation, so he can do in this case. The Work of Preparation does not make the work of the New Creation the easier; for after Man have a Work of Preparation, sin reigns in them as much as before; Preparation does not at all destroy the principle; and man when prepared, can do nothing to help God in planting Grace in them, and Men that are not prepared can do nothing to hinder God in implanting Grace. [*GC*, p. 5]

Briant and Gay told their parishioners that if they did good works they would not only be prepared but also could be assured that they would be saved. Stoddard told his that even if they are prepared, there is no assurance that they will be saved. And if they trust in their own works, it is virtual proof they will be damned. Stoddard chose to draw the battle lines around the old issue of the nature of preparation.

Stoddard said that "ordinarily we find that much time is consumed in the work of preparation," but he never tired of repeating that "preparatory work is no part of conversion" (*NSC*, pp. 12, 2).

> Men under the work of preparation are under the dominion and government of sin, their corruptions are stunded but not mortified, they are restrained but not killed, they are like Vermin in the winter, stupifyed but not dead. [*NSC*, p. 3]

Some intellectual understanding and moral improvement may come before actual conversion, Stoddard said. But he consistently refused to see any necessary connection between them.

For Stoddard there was only one thing that must come before conversion—total humiliation (*GC,* p. 76). An emphasis on humiliation characterizes the preaching of the true gospel minister.

> For men may see themselves as bad and insufficient yet not be brought to despair as to their own power . . . it is best to possess them with a sense of their utter insufficiency to help themselves; they may as well make a world as make their own hearts good; they can't work faith in themselves. They can't deserve that God should give grace to them. They can't force God to work regeneration in them, they have no natural excellency to engage God. . . . God is not bound to help them, there is nothing to hinder him if he pleases, there is nothing to oblige him, they can't compel God, God is free to help them, or deny them help, as it pleases him. [*GC,* pp. 69–70]

These sermons were preached in Northampton, but they were hammer blows against the theological tower being constructed in Boston. Briant, Gay, and Chauncy told men that the way to salvation was as orderly and smooth as the cosmic machine. If men improve their natural gifts, God would surely reward them with salvation. God was benevolent enough to design a scheme by which men might save themselves, and this scheme was as sure as the law of gravity. In such phrases as man has "no natural excellency to engage God. . . . God is not bound to help them," Stoddard must have spied out the enemy. He sounded a trumpet that would not call retreat.

Once the minister had men concerned about their own helplessness, Stoddard said he must continue to bear down. Enough is enough, Firmin had said; too much of the divine sovereignty was too hard to swallow. Chauncy and Mayhew refused to even taste what Thomas Shepard had called "the cup of humbling." Stoddard insisted men drink it dry. When a man is on the "very borders of despair," Stoddard said he should be told:

There is no hope in any creature. He can't help himself, he has no wisdom, power or worthiness that can help him; there is no way that he can take that is sufficient for his deliverance; that ministers are not able to deliver him, and that if others pray for him, yet they will not secure his salvation. All creatures are cyphers and can't work out any salvation for him: if God will destroy him, there is none that can save him. . . . If God destroy him he may, he lies at the meer mercy of God; if God will deliver him, he may; if he does not, he does no wrong. [*GC*, p. 72]

Stoddard reasserted the starkest doctrine of preparational humiliation found in Hooker and Shepard. When Increase Mather wrote the preface he tried to play down this aspect of his ancestors' theology. He said that Hooker and Shepard did not mean what they said in calling for total self-negation. Increase, although a son of the seventeenth century and certainly no Arminian, was writing for the new age. By sweeping the doctrine of humiliation under the rug, it was possible to hide the lines of development and deviation that ran between Increase's time and that of his forefathers. There was not much difference between Firmin, Hooker, and Shepard, Increase said; the founding divines did not really mean what they preached. But there was never any question that Stoddard meant every word that he preached.

But even Stoddard drew up short before the faith of the fathers. He refused to say, as Hooker and Shepard had said, that a man must be willing to be damned. It is hard to understand why he hesitated at this border that his grandson was to cross so decisively. He said that a man need not be willing to be damned, because it goes against his inherent principle of self-love (*GC*, pp. 64–65). But Stoddard, as we shall see, launched an attack on man's "spirit of self-love" unrivaled by any that came before or after him. He clearly thought the principle of self-love was an invention of the devil; but why did he invoke it only here, on this point? In the end, he said, it was enough that men submit themselves to God's will without being willing to be damned (*TS*, p. 58). But he concluded by asserting the very principles that led his forebears to demand of men the fullness of humiliation.

> Yet those that love God prefer his glory before their salvation: they are satisfied in the Wisdom and Justice of God in damning men for his honour; they desire salvation principally that they may honour God. They do count the honour of God of greater moment than their salvation, and take a complacency in that, that God will not dishonour himself but will glorify his name. [*TS*, p. 59]

Stoddard never forgot his commencement oration. These principles, if followed consistently, would lead men to be willing to be damned for God's glory. It would take a mind more concerned with consistency and less imbued with the spirit of Harvard to follow these principles to the bitter end. Such a mind was being formed in Stoddard's own lineage as these words were preached. Jonathan Edwards never went to Boston until after the direction of his mind was firmly established. He cared nothing for the spirit of Harvard and he took delight in wishing "to lie infinitely low before God." [8]

Stoddard was consistent, though, in his attack on the underpinnings of the new century. The scheme of salvation that men such as Gay, Briant, and Chauncy were gently forging in the pulpits in and around Boston was based on the equation of redemption with moral activity. They specifically rejected the idea that men merited salvation by the moral life; rather, they simply made the moral life synonymous with the state of salvation. Men were not saved by their works; faith was essential. But faith was the assurance that God would honor man's best efforts. This liberal soteriology was made up of two components: (1) the virtual equation of the religious life with the

8. Jonathan Edwards, "Personal Narrative" in *Jonathan Edwards Selections,* ed. C. H. Faust and T. H. Johnson (New York: Hill and Wang, 1962).

moral life and (2) the necessary commitment on God's part to honor man's moral life. The corollary of this was, as Gay and Briant were quick to point out, that man's works were not, as the Calvinists said, "filthy rags," but "shining stars." For it was man's good works that constituted, even if they did not strictly "merit," his standing before God.

Stoddard attacked both these ideas. Against the very foundation of the liberal system, the gradual coalescence of morality and salvation, Stoddard said: "The light of nature teacheth morality: the law written in the heart is the Moral Law. But Morally [sic] differs very much from conversion. . . . Moral virtues don't render Men acceptable to God, for though they look like Graces, yet they are lusts" (*TS*, p. 81). By making an equally sharp distinction between the moral man and the redeemed man, Stoddard brought to bear on his own time John Cotton's sharp distinction between belief and unbelief and Norton's sharp distinction between saving and common grace. Everything that Gay and Briant exalted in terms of nature and morality, Stoddard separated from conversion.

The other part of the liberal scheme was equally repugnant to Stoddard. The notion that man's duties have any bearing on man's standing before God was simply false. God is no respecter of persons; he does not note their pedigree or their Harvard degree. There is nothing in man that can make any difference to his salvation.

> Therefore they should be convinced upon what terms they stand with God; as there is no merit in their duties, so there is nothing to move God to pity them, nor abate the anger of God towards them; but their best duties are provocations, and imputed to them as sins. [*GC*, p. 42]

But even worse was the idea of telling men that God was bound to have mercy upon them.

> It is in no way fit to tell a man that God will shew mercy on him. For though this be the manner of God, when men are prepared for grace, to bestow grace upon them,

yet there is no promise in the scripture made to such persons; the promises are made to the coming of Christ; faith is the condition of salvation and there be many promises made to humility, yet there are none made to humiliation. And he is to be told that he is in God's hands, God is liberty to do as he will with him, and he must wait upon God to open his eyes and shew Jesus Christ unto him. [*GC*, p. 74]

The voice of John Cotton before the antinomian synod echoed through the woods of Northampton. Stoddard, knowingly or unknowingly, called the bluff of Increase Mather and the whole history of seventeenth-century New England Puritanism. He summoned the spirits of the founding fathers to testify against the heresies of the new age. It was Stoddard, with his stark portrayal of the sovereignty of God, and not Increase and Cotton with their moralism, who stood in the succession of the first prophets.

When Chauncy and Mayhew told people they were in the hands of God, they meant in the hands of a benevolent deity, who in his kindheartedness created the best of all possible worlds, one where men could get their heavenly reward as they got their earthly one—by earning it. When Stoddard told men they were in the hands of God, it was the God of Cotton, Hooker, and Shepard, the God who humbled men before he raised them, who was not bound to regard the works of even his rational creatures. At the turn of the century, almost exactly fifty years before Lemuel Briant held forth on "the absurdity and blasphemy of depreciating moral virtue," Samuel Willard issued his neglected warning on the dangers of moralism. Stoddard was not content to issue a warning; he issued a frontal attack.

His [man's] labour and service does lay no bond upon God to shew mercy to him. Whatever he has pretended in his prayers, he has no true regard to the Glory of God, he has minded nothing higher than his own salvation; he has been serving himself and not God. God is no ways obliged to give him such a reward . . . he hasn't merited grace . . . God has a liberty to bestow his grace upon whom he will. Mercy is God's own, and he will make choice who shall be the subjects of it. God is master of his own gifts, he will bestow them upon one and deny them to others. [*GC*, pp. 55–56]

Stoddard foresaw that some would call for a kind of resignation to the divine will out of a contractual concern that this resignation would lead to God's grace. Stoddard gave them no peace. He said men with such a bargaining mentality "have got a false submission." No man can truly humble himself, because even humiliation must be an act of sovereignty. "When men are brought to submit to God indeed, the thing is forced. . ." (*GC*, p. 62).

Even more than his denial that morality was the key to salvation, his refusal to countenance self-love reveals his opposition to the coming century. As our study has progressed we have noticed the gradual rise and acceptance of the idea that man is a creature of self-love and that this is good. From Firmin through Willard to Cotton Mather the central movement in Puritanism has not only been toward moralism but also toward acceptance of self-love as the spring of virtue. Willard spoke for the turn of the century when he struggled to identify self-love with God's glory, when he equated seeking man's happiness and God's kingdom, when he baptized self-interest as the proper motive for salvation. Stoddard spoke against it.

It is vain for natural man to pretend that they do things for Gods honour. . . . If they make themselves believe that their end is Gods glory, they delude themselves: and if they make others believe that they aim at Gods glory, they delude them: for they are governed by a Spirit of

> self-love and are wholly destitute of love to God. . . .
> They talk of aiming at Gods glory but it is only a pre-
> tense. [*TS*, p. 48]

Stoddard applied his basic distinction between common and
saving grace to this problem of human motivation. There were
two kinds of people with two kinds of motivation: natural
man was motivated by self-love, redeemed man by love toward
God. Just as common grace was not the complement to saving
grace, just as natural morality was not the complement to
conversion, so self-love is not the complement but the enemy
of love of God. Stoddard's prognostication of the signs of the
times was uncanny because again the assertion of these radical
dichotomies was a direct assault on the liberal vision that saw
only continuity between nature and grace, morality and conversion, man's interest and God's glory. That which Willard
tried so desperately to combine (which was his contribution to
the New England mind of the eighteenth century) Stoddard
tore asunder (*TS*, pp. 47–48).

> Natural men are under the government of self love. Godly
> men are under the influence of a better and higher prin-
> ciple, they have a spirit of love to God. . . . The first and
> great commandment is, to love the Lord thy God with all
> thy heart. But natural men are wholly destitute of this
> spirit. [*TS*, p. 35]

Firmin said that seeking salvation out of the fear of hell and
the desire for immortality was natural and human and to be
encouraged. This theme was taken up by the Boston liberals.
Mayhew often used the terrors of hell as a sanction for well-
doing. Even Chauncy felt constrained to define his universalism in such a way that it would not undermine the fear of
hell as the primary inducement to morality. It was one of the
ironies of the Great Awakening that, despite the sermons of
Stoddard and Edwards, it was the liberals who sought to
frighten men into righteousness by the terrors of hell. For

Stoddard and Edwards only the love of God would serve as motivation for holiness. For Stoddard the fear of hell was the prime example of self-love and not of true religion (*TS*, pp. 57, 60).[9]

Self-love, Stoddard said with his customary psychological insight, interferes with the total resignation required of the true Christian (*TS*, pp. 39–40). Men of self-love rail against God's sovereignty; they refuse to humble themselves before his judgments; they put themselves in a position of trying to understand God's inscrutable actions. In the end, Stoddard said, men motivated by self-love "hate God because he afflicts them in His Providences" (*TS*, p. 39). Self-love cannot be a motivation for redemption, because it is that which redemption is designed to overcome (*TS*, pp. 34 ff). God's afflicting providences soften men up for conversion by humbling them, but since the man of self-love will not humble himself under these afflictions, he can never even be in a position for conversion.

Chauncy and those who agreed with him felt that the desire for self-improvement and the search for happiness were the wellsprings of salvation. Self-cultivation would be rewarded with success in heaven and on earth. Willard said that in the same act men could aim at their own happiness and the glory of God; for Cotton Mather, Christianity was a guarantee of success. Both Willard and Mather tried to rekindle piety by calling on men to do their duty. Chauncy took them at their word and made moral duty and self-fulfillment the sine qua

---

9. Stoddard did preach a sermon entitled, "The Efficacy of the Fear of Hell to Restrain Sin." The point of this sermon was, as the title suggests, that fear of hell would restrain men from evil-doing. But Stoddard never suggested that simply refraining from evil had anything to do with conversion. Rather, he said that such "external" morality gave only external glory to God. Stoddard's distinctions between selfish motivation (e.g., fear of hell) and spiritual motivation, between morality and conversion, were not annulled by this sermon. Fear of hell might restrain evil and make society more moral and thus give external honor to God, but it would not make the individuals in that society any closer to being converted.

non of redemption. From the high pulpit in Northampton, Stoddard spied all the way to Boston and took note of these trends.

> Self-love governs them in their religion. . . . They may do all the external duties of religion, & therein put a great deal of external honour upon God; but still they have some selvish design in all that they do; they make the worship of God to be an engine to carry on their selvish designs; there is no love to God in those services. . . . Men aim at no more Religion than will promote their own interest. . . . Multitudes of Men, Act in Religion only from self-love, because they do oppose that part of religion that must be done for Gods Glory. . . . Those things that may be done for self-ends are attended but they neglect the rest. [*TS,* pp. 46–48]

This was not, as some have suggested, the reactionary outcry of the countryside against the excesses of the city. It was an analysis of a major cultural trend, if not the whole mainstream of American Protestantism. It was a call to battle in the first major cultural upheaval in American history. Stoddard would be dead before the troops would be lined up and the forces marshaled for war, but he would have passed on the mantle of the prophet and the reigns of command to one of his lineage and his successor in the church of Northampton.

Part Two

The New Age: Puritan Liberalism

7

Lemuel Briant (1721–1754) and Ebenezer Gay (1696–1787)

On the eve of the awakening, American Puritanism was already suffering from internal stresses and strains. Out of the original synthesis two conflicting trends developed in the course of the seventeenth century. The battle lines were drawn before the first convert fell into fits of salvation on the church floor in Northampton. The development toward humanism and moralism seems to have been powered by a dynamic within Puritanism. It would have continued with or without the event of the awakening and did not stop or even become diverted by it. It would have brought forth the attacks of men such as Edwards and Hopkins whether or not the revival had occurred. The final flowering of this trend broke into the open in Puritan liberalism, which was destined to become Unitarianism. A further elaboration of this trend will help place Cotton Mather and Benjamin Colman in an ongoing process of theological development as well as give some indication of the results of the movement that Stoddard prognosticated and against which he firmly set himself and his grandson.

The history of ideas rarely follows the neatly delineated lines of years and centuries. It is surely coincidence that, with the exception of Ebenezer Gay (b. 1696), all the men who subsequently broke with the Puritan synthesis in order to emphasize man's responsibility were born after the turn of the century. The same is true of Jonathan Edwards and Samuel Hopkins, who broke with the synthesis in order to emphasize God's sovereignty. The turn of the century marks a shift in the consciousness of New England Puritans, who were now less concerned with maintaining the tradition of the elders and keeping up the facade of unity and synthesis. Both the supporters and the opposers of the awakening left behind the ideal of balance and dialectic and moved instead into uncompromising assertions of God's sovereignty or man's autonomy.

Among the signs of this new age were Ebenezer Gay and Lemuel Briant, both named by John Adams in 1815 as having been Unitarians sixty years earlier.[1,2] Briant was born in Scituate in 1721 and graduated from Harvard in 1739. Harvard had become much more liberal since control had passed from Increase Mather in 1700, another event that shows the pivotal position of the change of centuries. Students were being encouraged to read widely and to scrutinize all positions. Colman complained, in the same year that Briant graduated, that too many "modern & new" books were being read there.[3] Briant was settled in Braintree in 1745.

He was twenty-seven years old when he preached, first before Mayhew's congregation and then before his own, his sermon on *The Absurdity and Blasphemy of Depretiating Moral Virtue*. Immediate controversy erupted between Briant and his more orthodox colleagues,[4] neither of whom compromised. Some of his parishioners became disturbed by the charges of heresy leveled against their pastor and in 1752 had a council called to investigate, but Briant refused to meet with them. They then offered to form a joint council that would include his supporters, but again he refused to cooperate. The council adjourned to give him time to reconsider. When it reconvened, Briant remained obstinate and so it went on without him. Charges were brought against both Briant and his wife, who were separated. The council did not address itself to these

1. Biographical information on these two men is drawn from *DAB* and C. C. Wright, *The Beginnings of Unitarianism in America* (Boston: Beacon, 1955).

2. Charles F. Adams, ed., *The Works of John Adams* (Boston, 1850), 10: 284, 287–288.

3. Quoted in Wright, *Beginnings,* p. 22.

4. This controversy is discussed in Wright, *Beginnings,* pp. 67 ff.

private matters, but it did condemn him for preaching some of the doctrines found in the controversial sermon, for replacing the Westminster Catechism with a more liberal one, and for recommending to his parishioners John Taylor's book attacking original sin. A parish council met and, in support of Briant, said that the right of private judgment allowed him the freedom to preach as he wished. They decided his doctrinal deviations were not great enough to warrant any further action, that his separation was more his wife's fault than his own, and they recommended charitable tolerance rather than censure. His vindication did not last; less than a year later he requested dismissal because of poor health and it was granted. He died a year later.

Ebenezer Gay was born in Dedham in 1696 and graduated from Harvard in 1714. He taught school and studied theology until he was called to the church in Hingham in 1718. He remained there until he died in 1787, having been in the same pulpit just three months short of seventy years. It is said that Jonathan Mayhew was a student of his, and through Mayhew, perhaps, Gay's spirit reached a wider audience. Gay did preach Mayhew's ordination sermon, in which he cautioned Mayhew "not to lean to your own Understanding . . . nor hastily reject any [doctrines] as false and absurd because they are infolded in mystery." [5] Such conduct, Gay said, would "ill become a young minister," but Mayhew was not one to take advice from even his closest friends.

In 1751 Justice Paul Dudley willed Harvard a fund for an annual lecture on natural and revealed religion, thus institutionalizing the concept of natural religion in the course of Harvard education. In 1759 Gay, the guest lecturer, spoke on *Natural Religion as Distinguished From Revealed,* and his Lecture became a *locus classicus* of liberalism. In Gay's Dudleian lecture and Briant's sermon on moral virtue, both delivered as the postawakening lines of demarcation were hardening, the logical result of the seventeenth-century tendency

5. *The Alienation of Affections from Ministers Consider'd,* p. 26.

toward moralism and humanism came into the open. Both Gay's lecture and Briant's sermon were seen by their contemporaries as major contributions to the developing position of the liberal party in New England.

Inherent in the liberal mentality was an elitism based on intelligence, breeding, and education, and it generated a disdain for those who did not, or could not, obtain a Harvard degree.[6] The reliance on reason meant that, for the liberal, men were to be judged on the basis of their adherence to reason's canons. Those few who turned out to be rational, and also by chance members of the same antirevivalist party, looked upon themselves as the epitome of humanity. For some, in England, the introduction of reason into religion was to have a democratizing effect. All men, supposedly, could read the book of nature, that "public library," for themselves and so have equal access to the new theology, but it did not work that way in New England. Briant was sure that the Christianity he preached, based on reason and "void of all corrupt Glosses and human Additions," [7] would appeal to only the select few.

> There always was and always will be some in the world (alas that there Number is so few) that have sense eno' and dare trust their own Faculties so far, as to judge in Themselves what is right. That by no Arts, how sanctimonious soever, can ever be bro't to believe (and much less Profess when they don't believe) Things repugnant to the first principles of Reason. [*ABD*, p. 23]

For Briant, theology began with the application of reason to religion. Reason exercised a critical as well as an explanatory role in theology and returned Christianity to what Briant

6. For discussions of the social philosophy of the liberals, see Charles Akers, *Called Unto Liberty* (Cambridge: Harvard University Press, 1964) and Alan Heimert, *Religion and the American Mind* (Cambridge: Harvard University Press, 1966).

7. *The Absurdity and Blasphemy of Depretiating Moral Virtue*, p. 23. Hereafter cited in the text of this chapter as *ABD*.

called "its native purity and Simplicity." Christianity must listen to reason's judgments so as not "to render it ridiculous in the opinion of sensible, thinking Men" (*ABD*, p. 23). The criterion for theology was whether or not it appealed to the educated gentlemen around Boston.

For Briant, one of the most irrational aspects of the evangelical scheme was the notion that man's good deeds are "filthy rags." "Neither all, nor any part of our Righteousness when true and genuine, sincere and universal, can possibly, consistent with Reason, Revelation or indeed so much as common sense, deserve this odious character of filthy rags" (*ABD,* p. 11). He insisted that he was not teaching justification by merit. He carefully emphasized that he spoke only about man's works after conversion, but the total effect of his sermon was far from orthodox.

The Christian's justification and his eternal salvation were not solely the result of faith or of Christ's work; they were primarily the result of man's morality. "It is the Righteousness of the Saints that renders them amiable in God's sight, that is the condition of all his favours to them, and the sole rule he will proceed by in judging them and despensing eternal rewards to them" (*ABD,* p. 20). Moralism triumphed over faith and the work of Christ as the grounds of man's standing with his creator. It is now men's works that render them acceptable to God.

Although Briant protested that he was not teaching justification by works, he realized that the orthodox doctrines of election, original sin, and salvation by grace had to be rejected (or at best reinterpreted) in order to maintain the position that it is man's own deeds that lead to salvation.

Hence it has come to pass that when Men read of Gods choosing whole Nations to certain Privileges (and these in this Life only) they have rashly concluded that particular persons are unconditionally chosen to eternal Life hereafter.—That when they have laid before them the

> Character of a very lose and abandoned people . . . they
> are induced to vilify humane Nature itself with the same
> vicious character.—That when they hear of our being
> saved by Grace, they conceive of it so as to destroy all
> moral Agency, and set themselves down with the vain
> thought, that nothing on their part is necessary to salva-
> tion, but if they are designed for it, they shall irresistably
> be driven into Heaven, whether they will or not.—And if
> they are not, no Prayers nor endeavours will avail. [*ABD*,
> p. 7]

None of the men we have considered suggested that man is
totally passive although some said that God is not under any
obligation to take account of man's works. What was new
about Briant was not that he strived to give man some role
in the order of salvation, for all the men considered here did,
but that he asserted man's "moral Agency" without any attempt to relate it to the divine sovereignty.

This alteration in the theology of conversion had profound
effects on his definition of Christianity itself. Since redemption
was synonymous with moral behavior, Christianity was synonymous with moralism. The reduction of religion to ethics was
complete.

> The Pure and perfect Religion of Jesus (which contains
> the most refined System of Morality the World was ever
> blessed with; which everywhere considers us as moral
> agents, and suspends our whole Happiness upon our per-
> sonal, good Behaviour and ever patient continuance in
> the Ways of Well-doing) is in many places turned into an
> idle Speculation, a mysterious Faith, a senseless supersti-
> tion, and a groundless Recumbency; and in short, every-
> thing but what in fact it is, viz. A Doctrine of Sobriety,
> Righteousness, and Piety. [*ABD*, p. 16]

Cotton Mather balanced his stress on morality and duty with
an evangelical thrust; in Briant the tendency to emphasize

morality and duty reached its climax. The first generation of men such as Cotton, Shepard, and Hooker balanced their concern for outward behavior with an even greater concern for inward disposition. Briant broke this inner–outer dialectic. The eighteenth-century liberal settled for outward behavior without even the lip service that his forefathers, at the end of the seventeenth century, paid to inward piety.

The reduction of religion to ethics is often accompanied by a redefinition of Jesus from saviour to teacher. Briant was no exception.

> Our Saviour was the great Preacher of Righteousness: For this end was he born, and on this grand design came he into the World, to propogate Truth and Vertue among Mankind. It is this and only this Righteousness (which some are pleased to style filty rags) which he preached up thro' the whole of that divine Sermon on the Mount; which contains the sum and substance of his whole Doctrine. [*ABD*, p. 17]

Christian preaching, then, was not the proclamation of Christ's atonement but the demand for moral obedience. Puritans sometimes defined the New Testament in terms of the Old and saw Christianity as a new kind of legal dispensation. Again, Briant completed a trend. The essential thing about Christ, like Moses a "law-giver" and a "Preacher of Righteousness," was "that he hath given us a most noble and compleat System of Morality, enforced by the most substantial and worthy Motives" (*ABD*, p. 29). The preacher was to follow Christ and "to explain and press the eternal Laws of Morality" upon his hearers. The test of Christian preaching was the extent to which the sermon made "all its doctrines subservient to Holiness," that is, the extent to which it reduced religion to morality (*ABD*, p. 30).

In short, for Briant, Christianity "is the sincere, upright, steady and universal Practice of Virtue" (*ABD*, p. 26). No Puritan, especially in New England, ever denied that the

Christian man was the moral man. That was, after all, the basis for limiting political participation to the saints. However, they felt that many could be moral without being Christian, and so they refused to define Christianity in terms of morality but instead conceived of it as an inward as well as an outward state. When men ceased to be concerned with the inner man, it was enough to define Christianity in terms of outward behavior. All the Puritans, even John Cotton, stressed that justification must issue in sanctification. Briant reversed this: sanctification issues in justification. In the course of the antinomian controversy Cotton expressed his fear that to take sanctification as an evidence for justification would soon lead to taking it as a cause of justification. The elders said his fear was groundless, but Cotton saw the future more clearly than they did. The road from the close of the synod through Giles Firmin, through Willard's warning about "preaching up moral duties" and Cotton Mather's moralisms, to Lemuel Briant's sermon was not such a long road. The Antinomian Synod meant a victory for those whose natural inclinations were toward duty and morality, and men such as Norton and Willard, to say nothing of Solomon Stoddard, could not stem the tide.

In his Dudleian lecture, Ebenezer Gay set out to discover the true relationship between natural and revealed religion. As we have seen from Cotton Mather and Benjamin Colman, concern for nature was nothing new in eighteenth-century Boston. As a matter of fact, it was nothing new in the seventeenth century, because men such as Shepard had argued that God's existence and some of his attributes were demonstrable from creation. When Gay proclaimed, "The characters of the Diety are plainly legible in the whole creation around us," he was standing well within this tradition.[8] It was not in his assertion of natural religion but in its relation to revelation that Gay represented a new thrust.

8. *Natural Religion as Distinguished from Revealed*, p. 6. Hereafter cited in the text of this chapter as *NR*.

Shepard had said that natural theology could serve as a support to revealed theology. Gay said just the opposite. "Revealed Religion is an addition to natural not built upon the Ruins but on the strong and everlasting Foundations of it" (*NR*, p. 20). Revealed religion must be based on natural religion and not vice versa. This meant two things: first, that revelation simply clears up what reason already knows on its own (*NR*, p. 31); second, that the propositions of natural religion could serve as criteria to evaluate the claims of revealed religion. Reason became the judge of revelation.

> No Doctrine, or Scheme of Religion should be advanced, or received as scriptual and divine, which is plainly and absolutely inconsistent with the perfections of God and the possibility of things. . . . No pretense of Revelation can be sufficient for the Admission of them. The manifest absurdity of any Doctrine is a stronger argument that it is not of God than any other evidence can be that it is. . . . To say, in Defense of any Religious Tenets, reduced to absurdity, that the Perfections of God, his Holiness, Justice, Goodness are quite different things in Him, from what, in an infinitely lower degree they are in man, is to overthrow all Religion, both natural and revealed, and to make our faith, as well as our reason, vain. . . . Revelation gives us the same (tho' clearer) Ideas of the Attributes of God which we have from Nature and Reason. [*NR*, pp. 21–23]

Revealed religion can only serve as a support to natural religion, which has become the test of revelation. God must conform to man's image of him (*NR*, pp. 22–23).

The essential character of liberal Puritanism appeared in Gay's discussion of the character of natural religion. Natural religion is a religion of morality because it tells man his duty and his obligations. Revealed religion, dependent on natural religion for its support, is automatically reduced to morality because that is true religion's content according to the dictates of nature. The purpose of revealed religion, then, is to provide incentives for man to fulfill his natural obligations (*NR*, pp. 6–8). "The Revelation of God . . . affords the chief assistance to our knowing and doing" the requirements of natural religion (*NR*, p. 8). The purpose of revelation is to reveal God's kindly benevolence toward those who fall a little short of their natural obligations. Revelation suggests to men "the Gracious Allowances He may possibly make, whose strength, so weakened as it is, cannot reach the height of their duty." The Puritan God of the covenant saw only sin in man's best efforts; the liberal God of nature saw and approved "the honest, tho' weak" efforts of his rational creatures (*NR*, pp. 18, 19).

Natural religion therefore bolsters the liberal soteriology of justification by effort. Like Briant, Gay rejected the idea that man's best works are but filthy rags and called them instead "a splendid and ornamental attire." [9] Justification, then, is a call to moral obedience:

> a special engagement to keep the Commandments of God —Effectual Vocation to be unto Holiness, and the operations of the divine Spirit therein, as not excluding humane Endeavours after Grace, or superceding all use of our infeebled Faculties in the Work of it. Justifying Faith as the receiving whole Christ, not dividing his offices, nor substituting his obedience in the place of ours. Perseverance of Grace, to be accomplished in a way of continual circumspection, and dutiful Diligence, working out our own Salvation with Fear and Trembling.[10]

This is the essence of the liberal order of salvation. Whereas the previous Puritans had said nothing must be asserted about man that mitigated the divine sovereignty, the liberals said nothing must be predicated of God that would weaken man's moral autonomy.

Revelation is built upon reason; grace is built upon nature.

9. *St. John's Vision . . . Explained and Improved*, p. 27; also pp. 26–28.
10. *The True Spirit of the Gospel-Minister represented and Urged*, p. 10. Hereafter cited in the text of this chapter as *TSG*.

Redemption does not transform the natural man but only improves and heightens what is already there.

> The Grace of God . . . doth not destroy a reasonable nature . . . but sublimate and refine it. It doth not obliterate but exceedingly brighten, what remains of the natural image of God, since the fall. It restores reason to its government over human passions, and directs it to its proper exercise.[11]

The implicit attack on the postawakening evangelicals is obvious. Grace makes men sober rational Arminians who know how to govern their emotions, not enthusiastic new lights. More important is the fact that where the Calvinists saw a gap between nature and grace, the liberals saw only continuity.

Under the liberal dispensation men are redeemed by their own efforts. The gospel consisted of moral exhortations and arguments to persuade them to put forth the effort. "Sinners are won to Christ and their duty by sweet invitations and arguments of divine grace. . . . [They] are not meerly affrighted or forced, but are charm'd into a surrender to the Lord" (*TSG*, p. 16). Giles Firmin's approach has finally come into its own.

Gay characterized the spirit of the gospel as a "harmless Spirit." This referred to the ministry but it was clear that Gay felt it applied to all Christians who "need be more inoffensive, than purity (alone imperfect) renders them" (*TSG*, p. 13). The real Christian must "give no offense" for the spirit of the redeemed "is a meek and gentle Spirit." Most importantly, "a man that has the due government of his passions . . . within the bounds of Reason and Religion" has the correct spirit of Christianity (*TSG*, pp. 14, 15). For the evangelicals, whose primary virtue was zeal, the Spirit was a power who transformed nature. For the Arminians, whose chief virtues were sobriety and rationality, the Spirit was inoffensive and kept itself within the bounds of nature and propriety.

11. *A Beloved Disciple of Jesus Christ Characterized*, p. 10.

It must be emphasized that these men, who sought to remain good Congregationalists and Christians, attacked the deists and atheists with as much vigor as they did the evangelicals. Their descendants would defend the establishment of the standing-order churches to the death. Above all, Gay insisted that liberal Puritanism must be founded on Jesus Christ.

> The church is indeed built upon him. And other foundation can no man lay, than that is laid which is Jesus Christ. He is laid in Zion for a foundation, a trial stone, a precious corner stone, a sure foundation. The church depends on him, as a building on its foundation. All the Grace, Peace, Consolation, and Salvation of it are founded in him, upheld and maintained by him. The Doctrine as well as the person of Christ is spoken of as the foundation of the Church.[12]

"Christ," Gay said, "is the Truth which Ministers are to Preach." [13]

Briant hinted at a separation between what the nineteenth century would call the religion of Jesus and the religion about Jesus. The seed of this distinction was being planted on the Continent by two contemporaries of the Boston liberals, Gotthold Lessing and Hermann Reimarus. Their work would become the basis of Continental liberal protestantism and the means by which later liberals retained the title of Christian. Gay did not argue this way. He said that "Ministers are to tell people of the Necessity and Nature of Regeneration." [14] But Gay conceived of regeneration in a very moralistic way. Briant told men to preach the religion of Jesus, that is, his moral code; Gay told men to preach Christ and regeneration, that is, the new life of morality. For both, the new birth became the new duty, and conversion became the process of moral self-improvement. The love of God was now the guarantee that man's efforts would be rewarded by salvation.

12. *Jesus Christ the Wise Master-Builder,* p. 6.
13. *Alienation of Affections,* p. 11.
14. Ibid.

8

Jonathan Mayhew (1720–1766)

Jonathan Mayhew was born on Martha's Vineyard in 1720.[1] He was descended from Thomas Mayhew who, having obtained the sole patent for the island, settled it early in the seventeenth century and ruled like a feudal king. He was also a missionary to the Indians, as were his son and grandson, who was Jonathan's father. Jonathan, who entered Harvard in 1740 when the revival was at its height, heard Whitefield preach to several thousand on the college green and was deeply impressed. Apparently Mayhew was involved in a group of students, who, touched by the revival, met together for prayers and psalm singing. A year later he made a special trip to York, Maine, in order to attend a revival. His report, in a letter to his brother, was fervent and evangelical, and he may have considered becoming a revivalist.[2] It certainly seemed that Mayhew was heading into the New Light camp. His father, however, was an opponent, and the influence of Harvard was firmly set against the revival. One can only speculate as to what might have happened had Mayhew's early piety received support rather than almost total rejection from his peers and teachers. At any rate, by graduation he was solidly behind the antirevival forces.

After graduation he remained in Cambridge to study theology and is reported to have been tutored by Ebenezer Gay. He was a candidate for the pulpit at Worcester, Massachusetts,

---

1. Biographical material for this section is drawn from *DAB*, C. C. Wright, *The Beginnings of Unitarianism in America* (Boston: Beacon, 1955), and C. Akers, *Called Unto Liberty* (Cambridge: Harvard University Press, 1964).

2. Wright, *Beginnings*, p. 64.

but a prorevivalist was called instead. In 1747, he was called, simultaneously, to the church at Cohasset and the West Church of Boston. The former rector of West Church had been reprimanded by Colman for doctrinal laxity, and he later became an Anglican and returned to Boston as rector of Trinity Church. Since the West Church was already known for liberalism and had a congregation of wealthy merchants, it was the obvious choice for one with Mayhew's theological and social sentiments.

There seems to have been a rumor of Mayhew's liberalism even before he was ordained. The West Church invited only two Boston churches, First Church and Brattle Street, the only ones with liberals on their staffs. Charles Chauncy and Samuel Cooper, the assistants at First and Brattle Street, respectively, were friends of Mayhew. But Foxcroft and Colman, the senior pastors of the two churches, apparently were not in favor of Mayhew and neither church sent delegates. Mayhew's father was delayed en route to the scheduled service, so it was postponed. No invitations to the new service were sent to the Boston churches; however, eleven country churches accepted, all the pastors of which were either liberals or Old Light, tolerant Calvinists. Gay preached Mayhew's ordination sermon and, as we have seen, advised him against outspokenness, but the advice was never heeded. Mayhew never became a member of the Boston Ministerial Association, and he was engaged in controversy most of his life.

He was a leader, as was the other liberal spokesman, Charles Chauncy, in the fight against an Anglican bishop. Mayhew's role in the American Revolution, which has been debated recently, is beyond the scope of this work.[3] A friend of Thomas Hollis and other distinguished British intellectuals, he was openly critical of the doctrines of the Virgin Birth and the Trinity and of any creedal standards for Christian profession. He died, unexpectedly, in 1766.

3. See Akers, *Liberty* and Alan Heimert, *Religion and the American Mind* (Cambridge: Harvard University Press, 1966).

For Mayhew, theology begins and ends with the goodness of God, which is the center of the Christian revelation. "The holy scriptures speak much oftener and far more largely and particularly, of God's goodness and mercy, than of any of his other perfections." [4] Goodness became, in Mayhew's mind, the key to God's nature; all other attributes, justice, sovereignty, etc., were subsumed under the category of goodness. Mayhew admitted that God is "in the highest sense, an absolute sovereign," but God does not act arbitrarily. He tempers his sovereignty in the direction of his goodness. "The Blessed God, tho' omnipotent, tho' over all, and not accountable to any, yet exercises no power, no authority, but according to his infinite wisdom and goodness." [5]

The same is true of God's justice, which like his sovereignty, is only an extension of his goodness.

> There are many persons, who seem to conceive of and speak quite differently of the justice of God; as if it were not a mode or branch of goodness, and comprehended therein, but an attribute distinct from, if not in a degree repugnant to goodness. [*TSN*, p. 20]

Defining God's justice and sovereignty solely in terms of his goodness removed the awe and terror that seemed an essential part of Mayhew's ancestral creed.

> What consolation can weak and sinful creatures draw from a consideration of those other divine attitutes alone, or independently of goodness and mercy? They rather inspire such creatures with terror and amazement, than with comfort, hope, and joy. Whereas, being considered as inseparably connected with goodness, which is equally essential to the divine nature, and exercised towards all the

4. *Christian Sobriety*, p. 51. Hereafter cited in the text of this chapter as *CS*.

5. *Two Sermons on the Nature, Extent and Perfection of the Divine Goodness*, p. 26. Hereafter cited in the text of this chapter as *TSN*.

> works of God, those otherwise formidable attributes, are, in great degree, stripped of their terror. [*TSN*, p. 19]

Mayhew lived at a time when the fear of the Lord could no longer be considered the beginning of wisdom. Now the thrust of liberal theology was to make God humane and benevolent.
    God's goodness is not only the key to his nature, it is also the key to his actions.

> The goodness of God comprehends his beneficence, or his good and bountiful acts, as well as the goodness of his nature. All beings act, at least in general, according to their respective natures, or the qualities inherent in them. And if the great God be supposed to be essentially good, it is hardly, if at all, supposeable, that he should not also do good. [*TSN*, p. 12]

God's, acts being rational, reveal his essential goodness for all to see.

> It is by what creatures do, that we form the best and surest judgment of their natures, qualities and dispositions, respectively. . . . We judge the internal characters and qualities of other men, chiefly at least by what they do; by their actions and conduct. And this is one way in which we arrive at the knowledge of the divine goodness. God "doeth good" and therefore we justly infer that he "is good," even essentially so. This way of reasoning is at once conclusive and plain, being accommodated to people of all capacities in general. [*TSN*, p. 13]

There are two important implications of this close connection between God's nature and his works, especially his work of creation. The first is that man can know God's nature from his works because reason, on the basis of what is given in nature, can know the essence of God without the aid of revelation. We noticed the same theme in Briant and Gay. Reason and revelation, Mayhew said, "mutually confirm and illustrate each other" (*CS*, p. 50). But this mutuality is predicated on making reason the judge of revelation.

Knowing God through reason is synonymous with knowing God through nature. Since Christianity was identified with what is "agreeable" to nature and reason, Mayhew had no trouble identifying religion with rationality (*CS*, p. 50). The "religious" was another name for the "sober" and the "rational;" and rational referred both to a man's character and his source of knowledge. Thus Mayhew, like Gay and Briant, exhorted his congregation to make reason the sole judge of their religion. "I would not, on any account, exhort you to do what is unreasonable in the least degree; either to believe things without proper evidence of their truth or to act absurdly and irrationally in any respect" (*CS*, p. 224).

It is interesting to note in passing that Mayhew's rationalism was combined with a certain kind of antiintellectualism. He attacked those whose minds are possessed by some "scheme of systematical divinity." [6] Although the Boston liberals manifested an implicit elitism of the educated, Mayhew condemned those who engaged in speculative theology because not all men can understand them.

> Are there not many Protestants, in whose yet unreformed and depraved judgment, hardly anything merits the honourable appellation of sound doctrine, besides the subtleties and refinements of speculative men, respecting certain obstruse and at best very doubtful points? Such as, one may safely say, very few people can ever understand, and fewer still were probably better for . . . especially men, who were hardly easy, but when they were either coining some new, unscriptural definitions and distinctions, in the ungolden mint of their own brain, or imperiously imposing this drossy counterfeit coin upon their neighbors. [*CS*, p. 12]

6. *Striving to enter in at the Strait Gate*, p. 46. Hereafter cited in the text of this chapter as *SE*.

Perhaps the sources of American antiintellectualism ought to be sought not in the emotionalism of the revival but in the learned attacks on philosophy by the Boston liberals. Mayhew certainly reflected what would become a common American impatience with thought and a tendency to subsume reflection under activity and morality.

> It is infinitely dishonourable to the all good and perfect Governor of the world, to imagine that he has suspended the eternal salvation of men upon any niceties of speculation: or that any one who honestly aims at finding the truth, and at doing the will of his maker, shall be finally discarded because he fell into some erroneous opinions.[7]

It is a person's character and not his beliefs that are important.

The second implication of the close conjunction of God's goodness with his works is that this is the best of all possible worlds. Since God's works flow essentially from his goodness, they too reflect and partake of that essential goodness.

> It is evident to sense and reason, that the whole visible creation is the work of a good and merciful being, not merely of a most intelligent & powerful One. The structure, the admirable order and adjustment of the various parts, nothing superflous, nothing wanting, from where results the harmony and beauty of the whole . . . loudly proclaiming at once the power, wisdom, and goodness of the adoreable creator. [*TSN,* p. 41]

As in Gay's Dudleian lecture, reason deduced that God is good because creation itself is good. The essential goodness of the world is the basis of reason's knowledge of the essential goodness of God.

Not only nature itself but man's own experience as well reflects the divine perfection. "Look down upon the earth, or to look round the world which you inhabit, in which there are actually innumerable infinite markes and characters of in-

7. *Sermons,* p. 103. Hereafter cited in the text of this chapter as *S.*

finite power, of the most consummate wisdom and goodness"
(*CS*, p. 54). This is so because of the unity of the divine nature
and purpose. Since God's intention is singular—to manifest
his own goodness—all his actions are directed toward this end.
Mayhew identified God's intention to manifest his goodness
with an intention to make men happy. Since this is the governing principle of the world, the conclusion is obvious. This
is the best of all possible worlds, that is, one designed for
man's happiness.

> As the natural and moral world are under one and the
> same common direction or government; so God's end in
> all things, however various and diverse, is really one and
> uniform . . . all tend to the same point at last; the moral
> perfection and happiness of the creatures capable of it,
> or the glory of God; which, in any good and intelligent
> sense, seems to amount to the same thing.[8]

This is the keystone of the liberals' edifice, the means by
which they sought to make Puritanism compatible with the
eighteenth century. Willard struggled to combine man's happiness and God's glory; the liberals embraced this and gave it
the central place in their theology. The chief end for which
God created the world was that men might be happy.[9] "[God]
is a being absolutely independent and self-sufficient, whose
goodness alone prompted him to give us existence at first,
and who governs us, not for his own sake, but only that we
may be happy" (*S*, p. 168). In the liberal Puritans the anthro-
pocentric tendency of the seventeenth century reached its full-
est theological expression. God was made over in the image of
man's reason to make him comprehensible to man. In order

8. *The Expected Dissolution of All things, A Motive to Universal Holiness,* p. 59.

9. Speaking of God's actions, Mayhew said, they "are not only holy and
just, but good; actually kind and beneficial in their nature, design and
tendency; adapted to promote the great end of his universal government,
the good of his creatures and therein his own glory; for these are inseparably connected" (*Two Sermons,* p. 77).

that he may not be a terror to the new humanism, the goal of all God's actions and the criterion of all theological judgment became man's happiness.

There is obviously one problem with this optimistic view of the world—the problem of evil. Men obviously suffer, and the question is bound to be asked whether this suffering contradicts God's intention. Mayhew, by making God's justice a branch of his goodness, provided the key to his answer to the problem of suffering. God does punish his people, but, as with all his actions, he does it for their own good.

> Shall we, can we really suppose, that He who is good to all, and whose tender mercies are over all his works, ever punishes his creatures without any good end, either in respect to themselves or other members of his household and kingdom? . . . To say that the infinitely wise and good God, punishes any of his creatures meerly for his own glory, without any regard to the preservation of order and happiness, and even contrary to the common good of those, to whom he was pleased to give being, appears to me at best very irrational. [*TSN*, p. 25]

Suffering, then, is sent by God as punishment but it is reformative and not penal. "Mankind in the present state actually need trials and afflictions, as a means of promoting their moral good and future happiness" (*TSN*, p. 58).[10]

For Mayhew, as for all liberals, man's condition was totally in his own hands. If man suffered, it was his own fault: his suffering was sent from God as a punishment for the misuse of his freedom.

> Most of the pains, both mental and corporal, which mankind suffer in this world are of their own creating. They

10. According to Mayhew the divine wisdom in providing discipline for men ought to be more emulated by human parents. "There are probably many more children," he wrote, "hurt, and almost ruined by the indescrete kindness, and excessive indulgence, than by the too great rigor and severity of parents" (*Two Sermons*, p. 79).

> are the natural effects on intemperance and other vices.
> . . . [They are] brought upon us by the providence of
> God for our own sins, to chastize and thereby to reform
> us, in order to our present and future good. [*TSN*, pp.
> 61–62]

This idea that man's fate was in his own hands tended to
reinforce the social elitism of the liberal vision. If a man was
poor or hungry it was probably his own fault. Mayhew also
held, as did most liberals, that the universe and society were
hierarchically arranged. Some, born with talents and abilities,
would succeed if they cultivated them. Therefore Mayhew advised everyone and everything in the cosmic order to be content with its place (*TSN*, pp. 30–31). If a man were poor, he
could be told that it was his own fault for succumbing to vice
and intemperance and that he should be content with his lot.
Those who were wealthy could be told that they should take
pride in their achievements and that they were chosen by God
to be aristocrats and successful merchants.

Another reason God sent suffering upon men, Mayhew said,
was to uphold his government. If God let sin go unpunished,
he would not be a very good magistrate. It is precisely because
he is good and wise that he sends afflictions.

> It is not inconsistent with the most perfect goodness, es-
> pecially in certain cases, to punish wicked men. No
> earthly sovereign is accounted the less good or merciful
> for punishing rebels, traitors and felons even capitally,
> when the support of his government and the common
> good of his kingdom require it. [*TSN*, p. 67]

God's punishment then is not vindictive, nor is it aimed at
promoting his own glory.[11] It is purely the logical result of

11. Obviously, his view of suffering and of the divine goodness lead
Mayhew to reject the doctrine of reprobation in unequivocal terms. "If
any persons really hold such a doctrine, neither any man on earth, nor
angel in heaven, can reconcile it with the goodness of God. . . . [This
doctrine] is most false and unscriptural, horible to the last degree, to all

the rules of good government. "Neither does he inflict any punishments, but what he considers needful for the support of his government . . . for the good of his people in general, by way of example and terror, that good order may be preserved." It is interesting that Mayhew approved of terror (i.e., the fear of hell and punishment) as an incentive to orderly conduct. For Mayhew, whether God sends suffering as a means to reform men or to uphold his government, it is all for man's own good. "Our heavenly father chasteneth and punisheth his children in this world for their good" (*TSN*, pp. 20–21, 25). Suffering does not mitigate but supports the liberal faith that God does everything to promote man's happiness.[12]

The idea that God acts to uphold his own government led Mayhew naturally to adopt the so-called governmental theory of the atonement. Other theories of the atonement suggested that Christ had to suffer because God's justice demanded some satisfaction. Since the liberals, like Mayhew, had made God's justice a function of his goodness and played down its role as a separate attribute, the doctrines of the atonement that made

---

men of an undepraved judgment and blasphemous against the God of heaven and earth. Neither is it possible for any man, who really believes what the Scriptures teach concerning the goodness of God even to think of this other doctrine but with great indignation" (*Two Sermons*, p. 66).

12. An interesting sidelight to Mayhew's faith that this is the best of all possible worlds despite the presence of suffering and death is his belief in animal reincarnation. Confronted with the suffering of animals, which seems to have no beneficial aspects, he speculated about their possible reincarnation. "How come you to know, that there is certainly an end of all, or any of them [lower animals]? Who told you that they do not transmigrate into, or assume other bodies successively, in which they enjoy life in a more perfect manner than in the preceeding state? Has God plainly revealed anything to the contrary in his word? No. Does reason discern any impossibility, absurdity, or even improbability in this supposition? Neither of them. Nay; there is some natural and positive ground of presumption, or a degree of probability that this is really true. It is certain that every living, sensitive creature is endowed with some principle distinct from matter . . . and this may survive the body, be continued after the dissolution of the present organs of sensation and live in another body" (*Two Sermons*, p. 60).

the satisfaction of justice a primary need were no longer relevant. Given the centrality of the divine goodness, one might ask why any doctrine of the atonement was needed. In part, the liberals did not want to break completely with their Calvinist heritage, in which the doctrine of the atonement played a large part. The governmental theory answered their needs perfectly because it enabled them to give significance to the work of Christ without emphasizing the divine justice.

> Sinful men, as such, need a mediator between God and them; a redeemer and saviour from sin and death. . . . It was not consistent with his [God's] wisdom and majesty or the dignity of his laws and the honor of his government . . . for God to overlook, or to forgive, the transgressions of men, without the intervention of a mediator; who should do and suffer what might have a tendency to vindicate the honor of his laws, by exciting and preserving in all a just veneration for his government, at the same time that guilty creatures were made partakers of his lenity and grace. [*CS*, p. 90]

As we have seen, by the time of Mayhew the governmental theory was nothing new in New England. As usual, the liberals did not invent something totally new but took an old doctrine and adapted it to their needs. The governmental theory had been used to uphold the divine justice, but Mayhew was able to use it to forge a view of the atonement without any reference to justice. In Mayhew's mind this theory shifted the ground of the atonement from the divine justice to the more "rational" ground of the order of good government. The atonement was no longer a mystery but rather an expression of God's rationality in that he follows the proper rules in the conduct of his government. John Cleaveland took issue with Mayhew and said that such an emphasis on the divine goodness made the atonement superfluous or simply a matter of convenience.[13] Mayhew was able to retort correctly that his

13. See John Cleaveland, *An Essay to Defend Some of the Most Important Principles;* see also Wright, *Beginnings*, pp. 217–222.

theory was nothing new and that he stood in a long tradition
of New England Puritanism.[14]

The idea that Jesus's work lay essentially in "supporting
the honor of God's violated commandments and the dignity of
his government" fit in well with the moralism implicit in
the liberal scheme (*TSN*, p. 49). The heavy emphasis on God's
law made Christianity a form of legalism. Man was related to
God through a series of commandments, and Jesus became a
new Moses, a new lawgiver.

> Jesus Christ came into the world, not merely as a light to
> lighten it with the knowledge of the only true God but to
> declare his will and commandments. . . . He came into it
> as a preacher of righteousness; to inculcate obedience to
> God's laws which were already known; to rescue others
> from corrupt interpretations. . . . He came to give man-
> kind the most perfect and engaging example of obedience
> to the will of God. [*CS*, p. 65]

According to the liberal plan of salvation, man saves himself
through obedience to the commands of Christ. The gospel lays
down the terms of salvation. Of the gospel, Mayhew said:

> Not only goodness, but even natural justice, seems then
> to require, that the terms proposed should be such as
> creatures in their situation, all things considered, may
> comply with, and so receive the benefit offered, providing
> they really desire it. [*SE*, p. 68]

What are the terms that man can comply with? In the gospel
God "has therein actually connected salvation with the endeavours of sinners" (*SE*, p. 72). If a man strives after salvation, he is bound to be saved.

The discussion over whether redemption is conditional or
contractual has involved all the men considered here. Some,
such as Firmin, suggested that if a man did certain things he
would be saved. Others, such as Stoddard, rejected any con-

14. See *A Letter of Reproof to Mr. John Cleaveland.*

tractual formulations of the plan of salvation. Mayhew drew on the former tradition, but he is enough of a Puritan to guard himself against the idea of merit. Men do not naturally have any claim on God by which their endeavors might merit their salvation.

> It is generally allowed that God is not bound in justice thus to succeed a sinners endeavours . . . to suppose that God is obliged, in point of equity, to do this, would be most absurd, not to say impious. For as sinners, we have forfeited all right to God's favour. [*ES*, p. 43]

Supporting this position is Mayhew's doctrine of justification by grace, according to which God accepts man's striving even though he is not required to do so. "Any certain connection between the endeavours of sinful creatures to obtain eternal life and their actually obtaining it . . . is a connection which free grace, or unmerited goodness of God, has made and established" (*SE*, p. 44). Mayhew went back to the claim of the elders at the synod: because it is free grace that establishes the conditions of redemption, salvation can be both conditional and free at the same time.

Salvation by grace was salvation by means of the requirements that God graciously sets.

> In short, to be saved by grace, meaning hereby the gospel of God's grace, is to be saved in that way, in that method, which the Gospel opens, provides for us, and prescribes to us. . . . In this dispensation of the grace of God, it is, we are assured, that Christ is become the author of eternal salvation to all them that obey him. [*S*, p. 118; also pp. 116–17]

It is an act of grace, Mayhew assured his hearers, that God redeems "transgressors upon certain terms therein marked out" (*S*, p. 116). The difference between salvation by grace and salvation by merit had nothing to do with works. Both require works on man's part. Salvation by merit demands perfect works; in salvation by grace God is content with the imperfect works of men.

> Tho' obedience is required in order to our salvation, it cannot be tho't meritorious of it. . . . Our obedience and good works are really acceptable to God in some degree; otherwise he would not have required us to perform them, and promised to reward them; as he most certainly has done. But yet they are not so valuable in their own nature, as to merit eternal life for those who perform them. God is infinitely gracious in accepting this imperfect obedience thro' Christ, and in bestowing eternal life upon the subjects of it. [*S*, pp. 113–114]

Salvation by grace is equated with salvation by works. (*S*, p. 112).

The central problem that confronted New England theology in the antinomian crisis had not been resolved even a hundred years later. Puritans still struggled to balance God's free grace and man's own efforts. Whereas the early seventeenth century struggled to find a place for man's efforts within the orbit of God's grace, the eighteenth century struggled to find room for God's grace within the orbit of man's own works. "However free the grace of God is, it is manifest that he has required something of us in order to our salvation. And our Lord here enjoins us to strive to this end" (*SE*, p. 23). The problem for liberal Puritanism was to try to find a way to affirm God's grace while asserting that we cannot be saved "unless we exert ourselves and strive in order thereto" (*SE*, p. 24).

The old Puritan idea, which could still be heard in and around Northampton—that God was not obliged to reward man's efforts and had not bound himself to do so—could not be exorcised from the New England mind by the simple assertion of platitudes about the goodness of God. The problem of contractualism had to be confronted and solved once and for all, and Mayhew tackled it with characteristic boldness. It was nonsense, he asserted, that God was not bound to reward man's efforts (*SE,* p. 66). The theology of such founding fathers as Cotton, Hooker, and Shepard was designed to deny any such contractualism. Despite the attempts of those such as Norton and Stoddard to hold to the old way, the tradition of Giles Firmin finally won out. God was bound to save those who performed the proper acts and obeyed the proper teaching. This contractualism, which some interpreters have taken as the essence of Puritanism, received full expression in the gospel of liberal Puritanism. "All who really desire and strive to obtain eternal life will certainly obtain it," Mayhew said, thus ending a century of debate (*SE,* p. 49).

The question of how much men should look to themselves, rather than look directly to God, in the order of salvation was fundamental during the Antinomian Synod. Mayhew was clear that man must look to his own efforts in his conversion. "Those who imagine that because we are saved by grace, obedience to the Gospel is not necessary, as the condition on our part, in order to salvation, draw a conclusion which is very unnatural" (*S,* p. 108). The question was bound to be asked, in light of the traditional doctrine, whether this allowed men to rely on themselves. Mayhew was never one to avoid an issue.

> If it should be objected that this doctrine leads men to trust to their own righteousness; I answer it is very reasonable that they should do so. . . . Good men may so far trust to their own righteousness, as to believe it will be available with a gracious God thro' the Mediator, so as to procure eternal life for them. [*S,* p. 167]

Now that the new age had arrived, Mayhew told his congregation that men ought to rely upon themselves.

The eighteenth century was not only an age of humanism; one could also say as Wesley did, that it was an age of "sanctification." [15] During the Reformation, Wesley said, justifica-

---

15. See Albert Outler, ed., *John Wesley* (New York: Oxford University Press, 1964). Wesley's rejection of forensic justification in his sermon on justification by faith is on pp. 198–220, where he rejected "imputed

tion had been emphasized. Now, in the eighteenth century, Wesley felt it was time to emphasize sanctification. The evangelical holiness of Wesley and the moralism of the Puritan liberals were two expressions of the emphasis on morality that were voiced in the eighteenth century. Both Wesley and the liberals attacked the traditional idea of imputed righteousness. Wesley said that this doctrine made men content with "no holiness" and that he favored the term "imparted righteousness," which means that God gives man a real righteousness of his own.

Mayhew too rejected the notion of imputed righteousness. Any righteousness a man has must be his own and not that of another simply imputed to him. He called it a delusion and a "grand capitol error" to say "that the merits of Christ's obedience and sufferings may be so applied and imputed to sinners, altho' they are destitute of all personal, inherent goodness." Mayhew, who, like Wesley, feared the consequences of such a doctrine, attacked those men "who place the whole of religion in faith and dependence upon the righteousness of Christ" because they "give countenance to vice and libertinism" (*S,* pp. 157–58, 107, 104). Whatever the scriptural basis or pious purposes of this doctrine, its consequences outweighed any such considerations.

> How greedily do many persons of licentious practices lay hold on such expressions as these, that we are "saved by grace," that we are "justified by faith without the deeds of the law," that we must be "found in Christ not having our own righteousness" and the like? Many vicious persons think they find great ground of peace, consolation, and hope in such-like expressions. [*S,* p. 102; see also *SE,* pp. 82–83]

These phrases, which were the watchwords of an earlier Puritanism, were rejected as a result of guilt by association.

righteousness" in favor of "imparted righteousness." See also his sermon "Ye are saved through Faith" (pp. 272–82) and his "Thoughts on Christian Perfection" (pp. 283–98).

Mayhew was not, however, ready to abandon his Puritan heritage altogether. Although man was saved by his own efforts, God's action still had a part to play.

> Whether a sinful creature can attain to true holiness and so be entitled to eternal life, merely by any endeavours of his own, or without the renewing and sanctifying influences of the Spirit of God? It is generally, if not universally, agreed amongst professed Christians, that repentance unto life and evangelical holiness are not attainable without the gracious operations of God's holy Spirit; and consequently, that without these divine influences, all the endeavours of sinners to attain to holiness, and so to eternal life, must be ineffectual. [*SE,* p. 42]

However, as Norton pointed out long before, the question was not whether a man was saved by grace (even the Pelagians affirmed that), but rather whether grace is common or special. Mayhew clearly felt that grace was common to all.

> If it should be asked, Whether any unregenerate sinner can be supposed to strive in the manner represented above? I answer yes, at least in general. There is very little, if anything, in this account of striving etc. which would necessarily suppose a person to be already born of the Spirit. But if it should be further demanded, Whether a sinner can be supposed to strive thus, antecedent to any influence or operation of the good Spirit of God upon his heart? The answer is by no means. [*SE,* p. 21]

The Spirit is common; it is given to all and it is up to men to make use of it. According to Mayhew's contractualism, God gives more of his Spirit to those who strive. "We may from hence therefore clearly infer that God will give his holy Spirit *to* those who . . . really strive to obtain life" (*SE,* pp. 68–69). The idea of preparation dropped out, and the natural man was able to begin the process of salvation as he is.

Since the process of salvation was seen in such moralistic terms, it is not surprising that Mayhew viewed the Christian life in the same way. For him the goal of all religion was to develop "Christian character" (*S*, p. 54). The "end of all faith," he said, is the development of "practical piety and virtue" (*S*, p. 106). Faith existed to serve morality; religion became simply a resource for human effort. "Christianity appears to be a practical science; the art of living piously and virtuously. . . . Those who do not learn of him to be sincerely good, learn nothing to purpose" (*S*, p. 83). The idea of Christianity as an art and of theology as a practical pursuit was nothing new in Puritanism. Derived from Peter Ramus, this idea was driven deep into the Puritan mind by men such as Perkins and Ames.[16] Mayhew took this traditional Puritan idea and used it to turn Puritanism into moralism. The liberals transformed the practical nature of Puritan theology into a theological precursor of American pragmatism. Whereas Ramists such as Perkins and Ames were profound theologians, Mayhew's pragmatism revealed the typical American impatience with thought. "Nor indeed is there any speculative error, however great, which can exclude a good and upright man, who obeys the laws of Christianity, from the Kingdom of heaven" (*S*, p. 105). For the early Puritans the practical nature of theology was not antispeculative but meant that theology was directed toward a purpose. For Perkins and Ames the idea of theology as the art of living to God did not mean simply living uprightly but also living for God's glory. In Mayhew the Ramist tradition, and all of Puritanism with it, degenerates into moralism. Even the Ramist homiletical form changed as sermons ceased to be doctrinal expositions and became simple moral exhortations to do good.

16. For the influence of Ramus on American Puritanism, see Perry Miller *The New England Mind: The Seventeenth Century* (Boston: Beacon, 1965). For the influence on Perkins and Ames, see Douglas Horton, ed., *William Ames* (Cambridge: Harvard Divinity School Library, 1965). See also Wilbur Howell, *Logic and Rhetoric in England, 1500–1700* (Princeton: Princeton University Press, 1956); Walter Ong, *Ramus, Method and the Decay of Dialogue* (Cambridge: Harvard University Press, 1958); Keith Sprunger, "Ames, Ramus, and the Method of Puritan Theology," *Harvard Theological Review* 50, no. 2 (1966): 131–151.

The liberals were not only concerned with morality as the goal of religion but also with the "incentives" to this morality. One of the most potent incentives, to the liberal mind, was the fear of hell (see, e.g., *S*, pp. 25–29). If one does not "strive" according to the liberal plan of salvation, Mayhew warned his hearers, one will be "excluded from heaven [which] is in effect to be thrust down to hell, where the worm dieth not and the fire is not quenched" (*S*, p. 25). Many of his sermons ended with exhortations to do good or to suffer eternal punishment.

> Perhaps you flatter yourself that the time of this dreadful exile from God . . . will be but short. . . . Far otherwise in the language of scripture, they shall be punished with an everlasting destruction . . . the smoke of their torment ascendeth up for ever and ever. [*CS*, pp. 303–306]

Unlike Chauncy, Mayhew seemed to feel this hell would last forever. But both Chauncy and Mayhew agreed that hell awaited all those who were not good. Both saw the fear of hell not as a motive for faith or conversion but for moral exertion. On this theme Mayhew could wax as eloquent as an Edwards or a Bellamy.

> Yet a little while, and he that shall come will come, and will not tarry. Me thinks, almost, I already see the heavens which have received him, opening, and the Son of man descending in great power and glory! the judgment set! the books opened! the dead raised! the righteous appearing with ineffable joy and triumph; the wicked with unutterable woe and anguish! both presaging, beyond the possibility of a doubt, what their sentence will respectively be! O, my young brethren, where were you? where shall I be found, when this day of the Lord arrives? [*CS*, p. 337]

For Mayhew, then, conversion became a process of character development, and piety and faith became resources for morality. Mayhew made even more explicit Cotton Mather's view of Christianity as a "powerful engine" for worldly activity and

success. The religious man is a man of character, the kind of
character that will bring one worldly profit. Being a Christian
is "most for your advantage in this world," Mayhew reiterated
(*CS*, pp. 257, 269). "It is most for your worldly interest to be"
a Christian (*CS*, pp. 259–60).

The liberals were terribly concerned about how they appeared in the eyes of their peers. They feared that the revivals
would bring disrespect to the ministry.[17] Mayhew assured his
hearers that by being religious, "you will also best consult
your credit and reputation in the world; at least in the opinion
of those, whose judgment is most worthy of regard" (*CS*, p.
241). The liberal gospel of Mayhew would not appeal to
everyone, but to its credit it appealed to the "best" in society.
"Which is most to be desired, the approbation and esteem
of the few wise and knowing, who judge of things according
to nature, truth and propriety or that of the vast multitude of
fools and mad men" (*CS*, p. 244). The liberal gospel, then,
assured one of respect in the eyes of those who count in
society. Mayhew does not hesitate to point out the material
advantages of this. "Virtue and religion will be a recommenda-
tion of you to the esteem of people, it manifestly tends to your
interest in this respect; I mean to what is commonly called
worldly gain and profit" (*CS*, p. 260).

In this gospel of worldly success, the providence of God
became the guarantee that those who strive according to the
liberal prescription will achieve not only heavenly bliss but
also worldly wealth. The contractual relationship between
man's efforts and his salvation is paralleled by a similar relationship between his working and succeeding in the world.

> If we suppose the Providence of God governs the world in
> a manner declared in the holy scripture; those who love

17. See Gay, *The Alienation of Affections from Ministers Consider'd* and
The True Spirit of the Gospel-Minister represented and urged; Charles
Chauncy, *Enthusiasm Described and Caution'd Against, Ministers Cau-
tioned against Occasions of Contempt, The Late Religious Commotion in
New England Considered, Seasonable Thoughts on the State of Religion
in New England.*

and serve him in sincerety, have much more reason to expect his blessing upon their honest designs and undertakings, in order to obtain a competency of the good things of this life, than impious and profligate man have. [*CS*, p. 261]

Mayhew began by redefining theology around the goodness of God. The divine goodness meant that God governs the world for men's happiness rather than his own glory. When this idea that the end of God's government was man's own happiness was combined with a view of happiness defined along the most individualistic and material lines, the conclusion was obvious. God governs the world so that men, at least the "proper" men, will achieve wealth and fulfillment.

It was not Calvinism per se, but rather the liberal gospel, that best corresponds ideologically to the development of capitalism in America. It lies outside the scope of this work to correlate the developing social history of New England with this theological history. Perhaps another way to view the developments within Calvinism during the seventeenth century that issued in the gospel of liberal Puritanism would be to view them as the development of the ideological basis of capitalism. The concern with man as an isolated and autonomous will increased the emphasis on his activity, duty, and reward. The new vision of the world was one made for man's success and one in which virtue and industry are always rewarded and vice always brings failure. All of these came to fruition in the liberal gospel and all of them correlate with the ideal of capitalist man—the manipulator, the earner, the bargainer, always looking for his just reward. Mayhew's list of the virtues of the Christian character would make a man successful in a developing capitalist economy.

Many of those virtues which belong to the head of Christian sobriety, have, in their very nature, a direct tendency to promote your temporal interest and happiness. For example: diligence in your worldly callings, temperance in meat and drink, and a virtuous moderation in other respects, have a plain, direct tendency to secure and advance your wealth, your health and ease. [*CS*, pp. 262–63]

The liberal gospel was well suited to the entrepreneurs of Boston who made up much of Mayhew's and Chauncy's congregations.

9

Charles Chauncy (1705–1787)

Chauncy, like Stoddard, was born into the aristocracy of New England.[1] He was the great-grandson of the second president of Harvard (his namesake) and the grandson of a Massachusetts supreme court judge. He was born in Boston in 1705 and graduated from Harvard in 1721, receiving his M.A. in 1724. He continued his study of theology and was called in 1727 to the Frst Church in Boston, a prestigious post, to be the assistant to Thomas Foxcroft. Foxcroft was as ardent a supporter of the awakening as Chauncy was an opponent. Foxcroft was paralyzed by illness in 1736, and Chauncy assumed more and more responsibility for this influential parish. By carrying the chief pastoral burden, he became well known to the important citizens of Boston who were enrolled there. Conducting funerals for prominent persons who were members of his congregation kept him in the public eye. He had ready access to the press and to sponsors, and many of his sermons were promptly printed. He usually represented the church at ordination councils and services and other occasions of state. Foxcroft was probably at least Chauncy's equal intellectually and was far more orthodox, but his influence waned due to his illness, and Chauncy was able to swing the strategic First Church in a liberal direction.

Thus Chauncy was soon in a position of power. He spent all sixty years of his ministry at the First Church and was chosen chief pastor when Foxcroft finally died in 1769. From

1. Biographical information for this section is from *DAB* and C. C. Wright, *The Beginnings of Unitarianism*. I have also looked at Barney Jones, "Charles Chauncy and the Great Awakening," an unpublished Ph.D. dissertation (Duke, 1958).

this bastion he was always engaged in controversy either over the revival, the establishment of an Anglican bishop, or, in the later part of his life, over the question of universalism. Unlike Mayhew's successor, much of Mayhew's former congregation, and several other prominent liberals such as Gay, Chauncy supported the revolutionary cause. Except perhaps for his universalism, he did not essentially add anything to the liberal thought of Mayhew, Briant, and Gay. But Chauncy's published writings are much more extensive than theirs and he was probably a more profound thinker. Thus he was able to give systematic expression to the gospel of liberal Puritanism.

Chauncy's theology was based upon what he called the "benevolence of the deity." Every theological statement must flow from and be judged by its accordance with God's benevolence. Colman, who began with the sovereignty of God, did not discuss God's sovereignty in itself but in terms of its manifestation in creation. Mayhew, who started from God's goodness, was more concerned with the goodness of God's creation than with the goodness of God as he is in himself. For Chauncy too, God's benevolence is not simply an attribute of God as he is in himself; rather it flows out from him into his works.

> Shall we not conceive of him as perfectly benevolent from the effects of his goodness we everywhere see in our world, and in all parts of the universe we have knowledge of? How numberless are the creatures he has formed with capacities for enjoyment? How amazingly various are these capacities? What abundant provision has he made for filling them with the good that is suited to their respective natures? And how emmense is the quantom of good enjoyed by them all.[2]

The cosmos is arranged hierarchically, everything having a place suitable to its own nature. When taken from nature and

2. *The Benevolence of the Deity*, p. 53. Hereafter cited in the text of this chapter as *BD*.

applied to society, this hierarchical model yielded the essentially conservative social philosophy of the Boston liberals.

One understands God in terms of categories drawn from creation. In order to be consistent, Chauncy must deny that God is essentially different from creation. Gone is the distinction basic to earlier Puritan theology between God as man knows him and God as he is in himself.

> Some, I am sensible, pretend that the goodness, and other moral attributes of God, are not only different in degree, but in kind likewise from moral qualities in creatures. . . . But this is a most absurd notion. . . . The moral attributes of the infinitely perfect Being, tis true, are incomprehensible. . . . But this does not mean that we know nothing at all about their true nature. . . . It appears then, upon the whole, that the goodness of God is the same thing with goodness in all other intelligent, moral beings. [*BD*, pp. 14–17]

Chauncy went a long way toward making God over in man's image, or at least in the image of the enlightened, intelligent, moral gentleman of Chauncy's congregation.

In order to bring God within the orbit of the liberal virtues, it was necessary to deny that God was his own standard of value. Rather, value was fixed; it was clear and obvious what was virtuous and what was not. God must conform to what intelligence, trained at Harvard, infallibly knew was good for the universe.

> Some may be ready to think that the will of the Supreme Being is the only measure of fitness in the communication of good; that what he wills is for that reason fit, and there is no need for any other to make it so. But this is a great mistake. There is, beyond all doubt, a certain fitness and unfitness, in order to the production of good, antecedently to, and independently of, all will whatsoever, not excepting the will of God himself. [*BD*, pp. 33–34]

Man's reason independently arrives at judgments as to what is good for creation, and especially for man, and then demands that God comply. It is no dishonor to God that he submits to the dictates of man's reason; rather it reflects his rationality and good sense that he agreed with Chauncy as to what is good for his creation.

> It may perhaps be thought reproachful to the Deity to have it said that he cannot, by a sovereign act of his will, constitute good, evil and evil, good. . . . There is such a thing as eternal and immutable truth; and it reflects honor, not dishonor, on the infinite understanding, that it will, and must, perceive this to be true. [*BD*, p. 36]

There are two important issues in all this. First, by establishing a set of truths outside God's will, Chauncy opened up the possibility of morality apart from religion. By implying that there are moral norms that reason can know on its own, he undercut his position that the value of religion is in providing the basis for morality. The liberal psyche never let go of the assumption that religion and morality are inseparably bound, and on this ground it fought the disestablishment of the church. By suggesting moral norms based on reason, Chauncy undermined this claim, and as a result, religion was pushed into the background. God became simply a servant and support for the morality man arrived at on his own.[3]

Secondly, Chauncy took the means–ends logic of Puritanism and imprisoned God within it. "It is," he said, "eternally and immutably true, that some actions are fit, and others unfit" to achieve certain ends (*BD*, p. 36).[4] Chauncy and Edwards differed over the end, the telos, of God's actions. For Edwards,

3. Mayhew too thought that God's sovereignty was circumscribed by man's reason. "The power of this Almighty King [God] . . . is limited by law; not, indeed, by acts of Parliament but by the eternal laws of truth, wisdom, and equity; and the everlasting tables of right reason" (*A Discourse Concerning Unlimited Submission*, p. 46).

4. Edwards held something formally similar in his discussion of "rectitude" in the *Dissertation Concerning God's Chief End*.

God's actions must be consistent with God's own nature and intentions; for Chauncy, God's actions must be consistent with what he calls "the common happiness" (*BD,* p. 37).[5] For Edwards, God's actions must be consistent only with his own glory. For Chauncy, since God's benevolence is directed not toward God himself but primarily toward creation, God's actions must be consistent with the good of creation. Some things, Chauncy said, clearly are not good for man, "and this must be known to a perfectly intelligent agent" (*BD,* p. 36). Having decided that the good of creation was the chief end of God's actions and knowing infallibly what is necessary to bring it about, Chauncy set about redefining God to bring him into agreement with this standard. God was defined in terms of benevolence because, for Chauncy, benevolence meant that God created a system totally aimed at the happiness of men.

Throughout the seventeenth century there was an increasing tendency to equate the divine agency with natural causation and human volition. Gradually God's act became simply another name for what, in fact, was happening. This trend took place at the same time that man was becoming more and more aware of the actual workings of the cosmos. The order of nature became sacrosanct and fixed as the expression of both the divine will and the immutable laws of nature, thus reinforcing the Puritan tendency to see things in terms of order.[6] For Chauncy, God's benevolent action was brought in line with cosmic orderliness. "The Deity does not communicate either being or happiness to his creatures, at least on this earth, by an immediate act of Power but by concurring with an established course of nature" (*BD,* p. 60).

This was one of the major and unresolved differences between Chauncy and Edwards. In Chauncy's world, nature revealed that God worked in orderly and predictable ways and

5. For Edwards, see *The Dissertation Concerning Gods Chief End* and *The Nature of True Virtue.*

6. For a discussion of the concept of order in Puritanism, see David Little, *Religion, Order and Law* (New York: Harper & Row, 1969).

made men orderly, rational, and predictable creatures. The disorder of the revival, in Chauncy's eyes, threatened the established order of the church. The conversion experience was not rational, and for Chauncy order and rationality were synonymous. The revival encouraged itinerant preaching, which disrupted ecclesiastical orderliness and encouraged men to leave their appointed social positions, thus upsetting the order of society. For Edwards, the world was one of miraculousness and openness, and God still worked in unpredictable and marvelous ways.

The logical result of Chauncy's theology, like Mayhew's, was that this is the best of all possible worlds. Since God's benevolent agency was practically synonymous with the way things are, the world must be just the way God wants it. Obviously, there is the problem of evil and particularly the problem of suffering. For Chauncy, since man is a totally self-caused agent, sin is totally the responsibility of man. Therefore, the problem of evil as sin is not a theological problem; it is man's problem, not God's. Evil as suffering does occur. Chauncy said that God sends suffering as a trial to be productive of greater character.

> The proper tendency and final cause of evils and suffering in this present state, are to do us good, in the natural and moral sense, or both. They are a suitably adapted mean to this end; and the all-wise merciful governor of the world makes use of them as such.[7]

The benevolent deity has created the best of all possible worlds, one in which men can save themselves by developing their character. The obstacles provided by suffering are simply incentives to men to grow and strengthen themselves. Rather than contradicting the liberal vision of the world, the problem of suffering is further evidence that the world is a trial through which men earn their eternal rewards. Also, defining suffering as a trial enabled Chauncy to defend universalism without undercutting the favorite liberal use of hell as a spur to

7. *The Mystery Hid from All Ages*, p. 324. Hereafter cited in the text of this chapter as *MH*.

morality. Hell is not eternal, but it too exists as a trial whereby those who did not follow the liberal order of salvation and develop their characters in this life can do it in the next. Thus Chauncy (and Mayhew) can exhort their congregation to avoid the trials of hell by enrolling now in the liberal course of self-development and the cultivation of virtue.

Gradually the focus of Puritan theology shifted from God himself to God's works and particularly to man. The debate between Edwards and Chauncy over the revival focused on different doctrines of man rather than different doctrines of God.[8] Chauncy's most original and creative theological work involved his understanding of man. If it can be said to be a mark of modern theology that it concentrates on anthropological rather than strictly theological themes, Chauncy was America's first major modern theologian. Obviously, the liberal soteriology demanded some substantial revisions in the doctrines relating to man, particularly the nature of original sin, the fall, and predestination, but these changes did not come instantaneously from the pen of Charles Chauncy. Before he was born there was increasing concern with the problem of man as a moral agent and with the relation of man's duty to his salvation; Chauncy used these trends to criticize the orthodox view of man.

His discussion began with an orthodox-sounding statement of the relation of Adam and his descendants.

> It is an undisputed truth . . . not only that the human race descended from Adam as their first progenetor, but that existence was communicated to them in his lapsed state; in consequence of which they have all along been, now are, and in all coming generations will be, subjected to a variety of evils . . . by the all-wise, righteous, and holy appointment of God.[9]

8. See, e.g., Alan Heimert and Perry Miller, eds., *The Great Awakening* (Indianapolis: Bobbs–Merrill), pp. xxxv–xliii.

9. *Five Dissertations on the Scripture Account of the Fall*, p. 129. Hereafter cited in the text of this chapter as *FD*.

The form of this statement echoes generations of Puritan orthodoxy. Man, fallen as a result of Adam's lapse, does not come into life perfect. This fallen condition takes place within the scope of God's plan. It was never Chauncy's intention to break radically with the theology of his forefathers. Except perhaps in the case of predestination, he proceeded by redefinition of doctrines rather than rejection of them. And the basis of his redefinitions was the doctrinal developments within Puritanism that took place in the course of the seventeenth century.

There is an ambiguity in the doctrine of original sin that plagued all post-Reformation discussions and that is beyond our scope to try to unravel. It is an ambiguity between man's nature and the guilt of his actions. What does man inherit from Adam? A corrupt nature and a propensity to commit his own sinful acts, or the guilt of Adam's sin regardless of his own behavior, or both? This ambiguity was to come to the fore in the discussion of imputation and original sin carried on by those who came after Jonathan Edwards.[10] Some theologians were content to plainly assert that all it is important to know is that man sins.[11] Others saw in the doctrine of original sin not only an expression of the obvious fact of man's wrongdoing but also an explanation for it.

If original sin is treated as an explanatory doctrine, some relationship must be established between Adam and his posterity, but this is just what Chauncy could not see. For him the developing stress on man as his own moral agent did not fit with the idea of inherited sinfulness.

It is a moral inconsistency to affirm that the sin of one moral agent can be the sin of another, unless he has been,

10. See Joseph Haroutunian, *Piety Versus Moralism* (New York: Henry Holt & Co., 1932). A good discussion of these issues is found in an unpublished dissertation, "New England Puritanism and the Disruption of the Presbyterian Church," by Earl Pope (Brown University, 1962).

11. William Perkins wrote, "Whereas the propogation of sinne is as common fire in a towne, men are not so much to search how it came, as to bee carefull how to extinguish it" (*The Golden Chaine,* in *Works of that Famous and Worthy Minister of Christ, William Perkins,* 1: 20).

in one way or another, voluntarily accessary to it. Adam
and his posterity being distinct moral agents, his sinning
could not be their sinning. This would imply a falsehood,
and a contradiction to the nature of things. [*FD,* p. 259]

Men cannot inherit the sinful actions of Adam nor, said
Chauncy, can they inherit the guilt of another man's sin. As
his own moral agent, man can only be charged with his own
guilt.

But this, without all doubt, is an impossibility in the
moral world. . . . We are incapable subjects of blame, till
we become moral agents; nor can we then deserve blame,
only as we charged with voluntary neglect. . . . Without
our own agency, how should it be possible we should be
blameworthy? [*FD,* pp. 160–161]

But Chauncy did not want to give up the basic outlines of
the orthodox doctrine that saw some relationship between
Adam's fall and man's present state. To both establish this relationship and preserve man's moral freedom required an act
of no little astuteness. In what was probably Chauncy's most
original moment theologically, he said that the first man
sinned and, because of the covenant God made with Adam, he
became subject to death for violating his side of the covenant.
It is this subjection to death, not any corrupt nature or moral
guilt, that men inherit from Adam. The main consequence of
the fall, he said, is "the subjection of mankind universally to
DEATH through the lapse of our first father, Adam" (*FD,* p.
138). How does it come to pass that Adam's death entails that
all men die? Chauncy had recourse to the same answer that
Edwards gave when Chauncy asked how it was possible for all
men to be constituted one person with Adam. Chauncy attributed it to the decree of God. "As Adam was the NATU-
RAL HEAD, root, or stock, from whence the human species
were to come into being, their subjection to suffering and
death became unavoidable, upon the judicial act of God
which condemned him thereto" (*FD,* p. 155). There is no

necessary connection between Adam's death and the fact that his posterity also die. But God's decree, his judicial act, makes men subject to death on account of the transgression and consequent death of their first parent (*FD,* pp. 158–60).

Chauncy profoundly analyzed the relationship between death and sin. The fact of death makes man anxious and afraid, so unnerving him that he loses his balance and perspective in life, falls pray to temptations, and seeks a false security. The fear of death turns him from God to the pursuit of self.

> It is easy to see, how all become sinners in consequence of their subjection to death, through the lapse of their first father, Adam. For, by his death, which should be critically minded, we are to understand not death considered simply, or nakedly, in itself; but as connected in the appointment of God, with that vanity, toil, sorrow and suffering, by which it is occassioned, and with which it is accompanied, invariably, in a less or greater degree, with respect to all mankind. . . . [It is] the whole disadvantage under which we hold life since the fall. . . . Now, the exitements to sin, or the temptations by which we are overcome to commit it, do principally follow upon our being thus in this sense subjected to death; that is, they are, in great measure, owing to the situation and circumstance of our mortal bodies in this state of toil and sorrow, which ends in the destruction of life. From hence arrise those fears, with respect to the loss of life which are so great an occasion of sin, in all its various kinds; from hence arise that impatience and discontent, that anxious solicitude and perplexing concern, which render life far more burdensome than it is derived to us from the simple constitution of God. From hence arise the earnest persuits of men, in every unlawful way. [*FD,* pp. 274–76]

Chauncy tended to be more concerned with the selfishness of the lower classes than with that of his own wealthy parishioners. Still, his analysis of the relationship of finitude to temptation and of anxiety to selfishness is (if we may speak anachronistically) worthy of the best tradition of existentialist theology.[12]

For Chauncy it is man's life situation, not his nature, that is fallen.

> This now leads us to a clear and just idea of the real circumstances of his [Adam's] posterity in consequence of his lapse. We come into existence, and live on this earth, not as it was in its primitive state, but as now lies under the curse of God; that is, adapted to render life, as long as it lasts, a scene of labour, vanity, and sorrow. [*FD*, p. 146]

The fall is not sin but the temptation to sin. Man's integrity is not corrupt, but the existential circumstances of his life are. By the divine decree, men inherit from Adam a world that tempts them to sin almost beyond their endurance.

This was a brilliant move on Chauncy's part, not only because of its analysis of finitude and suffering, but also because he saved the form of orthodox doctrine along with liberal theology. As in orthodoxy, Adam's fall bears a divinely decreed causal relationship to man's present state. But man's integrity and freedom are not morally vitiated, because he is still in a position where he can save himself.

The fall, then, explains the character of existence as the liberal perceived it. The fallen state of existence gives man temptations to overcome and obstacles to surmount in order to improve his character and earn his heavenly reward(s). "The posterity of Adam, notwithstanding his lapse, or the consequences of it, comes into existence under an establishment of grace, putting them upon trial for an eternal, happy life after death" (*FD*, pp. 200–01). The fall causes the suffering

12. Compare this with the discussion of the fall and original sin in Reinhold Niebuhr, *The Nature and Destiny of Man* (New York: Scribner's, 1941), 1: chaprs. 6–10 and Paul Tillich, *Systematic Theology*, (Chicago: University of Chicago Press, 1957), 2: 29–58.

in man's existence, but when combined with his view of suffering as the precondition of character improvement, it becomes a happy fall. It puts man, in this best of all possible worlds, in exactly the position the liberal thinks he should be—where he must work for his eternal salvation.

In all of this, man is an isolated, autonomous agent. We came into being, Chauncy said, "absolutely dependent on ourselves" (*FD*, p. 161). This is also the presupposition of laissiz-faire capitalism. As we suggested when discussing Mayhew, it is the liberal doctrine of man and not the Calvinist one that best corresponds to the rise of capitalism in this country. The liberal order of salvation is the myth of American capitalism, the myth of the self-made man, translated into theological terms. Chauncy must attack the doctrine of the imputation of Adam's guilt and the transmission of his sinful nature. To accept such a doctrine would undermine the individualistic nature of moral agency on which his whole system was based. "We cannot be conscious of any fault, unless we have PERSONALLY done that which is wrong" (*FD*, p. 152). Chauncy must maintain at all costs the personal, autonomous, agency of man.

This is why the debate over the freedom of the will was so important. Edwards's attack on Arminianism was not a piece of idiosyncratic theologizing but was an attack on the development of American culture that is based on the myth of the self-made man. For Chauncy the issue in this debate was to safeguard the vision of man as an autonomous moral agent, a vision that not only allowed man freedom in some abstract sense but, more importantly, allowed him to take credit for his actions. To be the cause of one's actions meant that one deserves what one earns (*BD*, p. 136). Freedom of the will meant, for Chauncy, the capacity to earn one's reward on earth and in heaven, thus giving man the right to his self-conceit (*BD*, pp. 29, 128, 136).

> It [free-will] is indeed the most important one we are
> endowed with, and the only basis of the highest happiness,

in kind, we are made capable of enjoying. . . . They [lower animals] have no perception of self-approbation, from a consciousness of having done well nor of the pleasure that is the natural result there from. This, perhaps, is the highest kind of pleasure communicable from the Deity; and it is perceivable only by moral agents. No beings, to whom the Deity has not committed the care of governing their faculties, can, by the exercise of them, deserve the applause of their own hearts, and enjoy the sublime satisfaction arising here from: But it is in reach of the capacity of all such to feel this self-approbation, and consequent pleasure; and they may go on in this enjoyment with continually increasing degrees, in proportion to the degrees of virtue they discover in the good government of these various faculties. [*BD,* pp. 137–38]

Probably nothing is more indicative of the liberal temper than this vision of man's highest pleasure coming from his own self-gratification. In contrast to the Puritanism of earlier days, Chauncy not only refused to condemn pride but also made the increase of pride the highest virtue.

For Chauncy, man does not come into the world as a fallen creature who must be reclaimed but rather as a potentiality that must be actualized. Although the fall does not affect man's constitution but only his existence, man does not come into the world already perfect. If man were born perfect he would not need redemption, and Arminianism was definitely a religion of redemption. Instead, man is born imperfect but perfectable, with the potential for perfection that his own efforts may actualize. "The posterity of Adam come into existence with implanted capacities, or principles, in the due use of which they may attain to a moral likeness to God." [13]

Even Adam, Chauncy said, was not created perfect but in potential. The image of God in which Adam, and his posterity, were created was not "a present actual perfect likeness to the

13. *Twelve Sermons,* p. 203. Hereafter cited in the text of this chapter as *TS.*

Diety . . . but a capacity planted in his nature, making this obtainable" (*FD*, p. 40). Adam was not perfect, Chauncy said, for if he were how could he have sinned. Rather, he was created with a potential and was put in a situation of trial that he failed (*FD*, pp. 52 ff). Thus the fall was not a drop from perfection to imperfection but simply Adam's failure to use his capabilities and his reaping the consequences of disobeying God. The fall, then, is not the precondition of redemption, since Adam, too, needed redemption (i.e., the improvement of his potential). The consequence of the fall is that man's redemption is made more difficult.

Therefore, Adam, created only as a potential, is a model of all men. "Man was made at first with capacities only," but by cultivation, "by use and exercise in due time," he might have improved these capabilities (*FD*, p. 30). The image of God, which (according to Chauncy) was not lost by the fall but rather which all men share with Adam, is "their being made intelligent, moral beings, capable in consequence of a right use of their implanted powers, of resembling the Deity in knowledge, holiness, and happiness" (*FD*, p. 35).[14] So, too, Adam's posterity came into the world "with nothing more than naked capacities," in the same condition as Adam. (*FD*, p. 23).

Redemption, then, becomes the self-cultivation of one's potential. Chauncy's theology of the nature of the fall and of the *imageo dei* fits brilliantly with the Arminian soteriology of self-improvement and the liberal faith in education and culture as the means of grace.

> This method of man's attaining to the perfection he was made for, affords not only the most natural occasion for the various exercise of his implanted powers, but constantly presents the most reasonable call for this exercise. . . . For these improvements, in all their degrees, in the

14. Chauncy elsewhere says the image of God is not "an actual, present, wisdom, holiness or happiness but [is] implanted powers perfectly adjusted to each other, and as perfectly fitted for his gradual attaining to this likeness . . ." (*Five Dissertations*, p. 62).

present view of them, are at once the result of the due use of implanted powers and the reward of the use of them. [*FD,* pp. 32–33]

Redemption coincides with moral self-realization, which is something man can acheve by his own efforts. Chauncy's discussion of original sin, the fall, and the image of God gave consistent theological foundation to the Arminian soteriology we saw outlined in Mayhew, Briant, and Gay.

Man does not earn his salvation in terms of meriting it. Chauncy and the liberals constantly denied that they taught a papist doctrine of merit. Rather, the liberals simply redefined the nature of redemption in such a way that the question of merit was no longer relevant. By making redemption a state of moral perfection into which man can develop himself, the question of merit never arose. Man does indeed redeem himself, but he does not merit this redemption at the hands of some deity. Rather, he achieves it all on his own.

It is by the intervention of ourselves, in great measure, that we come to the enjoyment of that happiness our implanted capacities tend to. The good we are originally formed for is put very much into our own power; in so much that we are more or less happy, in consequence of our own conduct. . . . The increase, especially of our mental and moral capacities is also put into our own power, that it is, in a great measure dependent on ourselves, whether they attain any considerable degrees either of perfection or happiness. [*BD,* pp. 61–62]

The corollary of this was obvious to Chauncy. Some men are unhappy, miserable, or poor because they did not have the fortitude and discipline to improve themselves. Chauncy continued:

A great part of mankind do not arrive to that extent either of perfection or happiness, their original capacities would have allowed of, and they might have attained to

had they more wisely fallen in with the tendency of that
general law, which makes their perfection and happiness
so much dependent on themselves. They do not use their
own powers, in order to their own good, as they might do,
and so come short of that degree of good this general law
tended to produce, and would have actually produced had
it not been their own fault. [*BD*, p. 62]

Chauncy may have arrived at a theology of redemption more
compatible with the eighteenth-century American mentality
than with that of orthodox Calvinism, but he did so at the
price of making Horatio Alger the model of the redeemed
man.

Chauncy himself offered the best summary of the liberal
soteriology when he described what he meant by the "new
birth" in contrast to the evangelical order of salvation.

Far from denying the Doctrines of the "New Birth" I
entirely acquiesce in it as a supreme one, highly important. . . . As we first come into being . . . our powers
are naked capacities only, which, as they gradually unfold
and gain strength, will, by their good or bad improve-
ments, acquire different moral qualities, giving us an
answerably different character. If our natural powers are
neglected, misimproved, and turned aside from their
proper use, we become morally corrupt and sinful; but
if they are cultivated and improved to our own attaining
an actual likeness to God in knowledge, righteousness and
true holiness, we may have now a new nature superin-
duced, and may, figuratively speaking, be said to be new
born creatures. . . . In consequence of a good education,
animated by the superintending influence of the divine
Spirit, they become possessed of those morally good qualities, on account of which men are called "born of God."
[*FD*, pp. 186–87]

Moralism had been introduced to Boston long before
Chauncy was born. No less a Puritan than Cotton Mather

made man's duty and moral improvement the focus of his preaching. It was not the invention of the liberals; rather, they were the product of a long line of development in that direction. Chauncy's originality was that he redid all Puritan theology to arrive at a doctrine of man whereby man is able to make himself into whatever he becomes. Chauncy reintroduced into Protestantism the idea that man becomes good by doing good deeds, the idea that Luther found most abhorrent in medieval Catholicism. When his idea of man as an almost limitless potentiality was joined with the idea that this is the best of all possible worlds, a boundless optimism is born that has characterized liberalism ever since.

> It is in consequence of this progressive capacity, that we suppose, and I do think, upon just and solid grounds, that all intelligent, moral beings, in all worlds, are continually going on, while they suitably employ and improve their original faculties, from one degree of attainment to another; and hereupon from one degree of happiness to another, without end. [*FD*, p. 33]

There were two steps involved in the liberal redefinition of the order of salvation. The first was to show that moral perfectability was obtainable by human effort. This Chauncy undertook in his discussion of the fall, original sin, and the image of God. The second step was to identify this state of moral self-development with the state of justification. Many generations of preachers had decried as pure hypocrisy the belief that the moral man was the saved man. Never intending to break with Protestant Christianity, Chauncy maintained the central Protestant category of justification by faith. Chauncy felt that the religion of Christ was the only true religion and never asserted that the morally upright pagan would be saved by his morality alone. Faith in Jesus Christ was a necessary condition for salvation. What Chauncy did was to make faith and morality equal and mutually dependent conditions of justification. Chauncy maintained belief in the necessity of Christ's work for man's redemption.

> Next to the Grace of God, it gives all due honor to the
> Merits of the Lord JESUS CHRIST. Tis with a view to him,
> for his sake, and on his account, that the Sinner is spoken
> of as justified and saved. These great, Gospel favours are
> granted him, not for any works of righteousness which he
> has done, but in consideration of the mediatorial Per-
> formances and sufferings of the Lord Jesus Christ.[15]

Men, Chauncy said, cannot be justified by works apart from
Christ, because Christ's mediation is essential to justification.

For Chauncy, faith was not the cause of justification but, in
words that echoed Willard and Mather, it was the "medium"
through which men receive the benefits of Christ (*TS*, pp. 158–
59). Although he did call faith a work, it was not a work in
the sense of something that has transforming power in itself.
Faith, in good Puritan fashion, only functioned in relation to
Christ.

> The sinner is put into a justified state, neither by his faith,
> separate from the obedience and blood of Christ; nor by
> the blood and obedience of Christ, separate from his
> faith. They both of them have their part and use in this
> business; nor can it be accomplished without their joint
> concurrence. [*TS*, p. 166]

So far then Chauncy's understanding of faith was continuous
with his Puritan heritage.

From the defeat of Cotton at the synod through the turn of
the century there was an increasing tendency to see faith as
active. Although some used the rhetoric of a more passive faith
and all maintained that faith was a gift of God, in fact, faith
began to function more and more actively in the order of
salvation. Chauncy's definition of faith was the logical result
of this development. Swept aside were the subtle distinctions
between the act and habit of faith, or two stages of faith that

---

15. *Ministers Cautioned against Occasions of Contempt*, p. 31. Hereafter cited in the text of this chapter as *MC*.

characterized previous theologies and by means of which previous theologians attempted to balance the active and passive
elements in faith. Such thinkers had felt the need to balance
the sovereignty of God (which seemed to demand a passive
faith) and the agency of man (which seemed to demand an
active one). Chauncy, whose only need was to assert the agency
of man, allowed no passivity in the order of salvation. "Nor
are men passive in this work," he told his congregation (*FD*,
p. 248). Climaxing the tendency toward an active faith is
Chauncy's bold assertion that faith is a work.

> It will, probably, be objected against this . . . if we are
> justified by faith and faith is a work, we are justified by
> "a work of our own" and not by the "work of Christ".
> . . . I would so far prevent myself, as to say at present,
> tho' instead of denying faith to be a work, I avow it to be
> one. . . . Nothing is more indubitably clear and certain,
> than that faith partakes of all the properties of a work.
> [*TS*, pp. 121, 124]

For Chauncy, faith was primarily assent of the mind. A more
and more external definition of faith in terms of intellect and
duty had developed in Puritanism in the course of the seventeenth century. The centrality of the intellect in the human
personality played an important part in Chauncy's anthropology and in his dispute with Edwards over the revivals.
Relying heavily on education in the development of human
potentiality, Chauncy came to an intellectualized understanding of faith. Faith was understood on analogy with knowledge.

> Faith and knowledge both [agree] in the assent of the
> mind to apprehended truth. . . . The assent of the mind
> in faith is gained in one way; in knowledge another. Faith
> is the minds assent upon testimony; and upon the testi-
> mony of God, if the faith is Christian. [*TS*, p. 71]

The Age of Reason changed the context in which faith was
discussed. Traditionally faith was discussed as a soteriological

matter, in relation to the order of salvation. After the incursion of the Age of Reason the context shifted to the epistemological problem, the issue becoming faith's claim to knowledge. Chauncy grasped this shift and solved both problems with one stroke. He combined the soteriological and epistemological problems by making epistemic faith into saving faith. He took over the modern understanding of faith as a form of knowledge and applied it to the traditional problem. Saving faith became intellectual, knowledgeable faith. "There can't be faith where there is not the assent of the mind; and where ever the assent of the mind is, there is faith, also" (*TS*, p. 83).

Chauncy continued:

> Tho' I must add, not always a faith that will argue a justified state; which ought very carefully to be remembered. Tis not simply a man's being persuaded the report of the Gospel is true, that will denominate him a justified believer. [*TS*, p. 83] [16]

Saving faith, by definition intellectual assent, was also primarily propositional knowledge.

> The truths contained in the revelation of God, considered in one collective view, are the proper object of faith. And he that is a believer, if his belief is such as bespeaks his being in a justified state, assents to all these truths, so far as his understanding extends. [*TS*, p. 82]

The key to saving faith was assent based on God's testimony rather than on culture or habit.

> The "ground" or "reason" of it [saving faith] is the witness of God. He sees God speaking in the sacred scrip-

16. On the subject of justifying faith, Chauncy can sound almost evangelical. "And yet [the Christians of the day] are far from being the subject of a faith that justifies. And the reason is because the assent of their minds to the report of the Gospel is not of the right kind. Tis the production of education and tradition rather than the testimony of God. . . . They receive the great doctrines of Christianity as speculations, not important realities" (*Twelve Sermons*, p. 92).

tures, and admits the doctrines there contained into his mind as undoubted verities, because testified to as such by the faithful God. . . . The man, whose faith is saving, has this view of them [the Scriptures] and actually sees and hears God speaking in them, which is not the case where the faith is only common. [*TS*, pp. 96–97]

Chauncy stood firmly in the tradition of Calvin and English Puritanism when he used Calvin's dialectic of Word and Spirit to define saving faith.

Since faith was a human act of intellectual understanding, it was something men can come to on their own, although Chauncy sometimes implied that a Harvard degree was a means of grace in this instance. This definition of faith reinforced the liberal idea of salvation as being up to man's initiative. The title of one of Chauncy's sermons is "Human Endeavours in the Use of Means, the Way in Which Faith is Obtained" (*TS*, p. 181). Because the fall has not touched man's nature, his reasoning power is intact and can be employed in arriving at the true understanding that constitutes saving faith.[17]

17. Chauncy's view of faith as assent and of the Scriptures as intellectual propositions for such assent, when combined with the idea that man's reason can come to the correct knowledge of Scripture, produced a theology not unlike that of the so-called Princeton theology of Alexander, Hodge, and Warfield in the next century. Their apologetics were based on the idea of external proofs for the divine truth of Scriptures, proofs that reason could know apart from faith. Chauncy favors the same approach. Natural men, he says, "may, by care, in the exercise of their reason, under the common blessing of God, be persuaded of the truth of natural religion, so may they, by like care, in the use of the same faculty, under the ordinary influence of heaven, become believers in revelation. . . . The evidences in proof of revelation lie open to inquiry by all, who are favored with the knowledge of them. And sinners, who are thus favored, may, if they please, attend to them and examine them with a becoming care and deligence . . . and become possest of a real faith in revelation" (*Twelve Sermons*, pp. 207–208). Perhaps when Chauncy was given an honorary degree at the institution of which Edwards had been named president, it revealed not only the drastic changes in Princeton under the direction of Witherspoon, but also signaled the future course of

> Sinners, tho' destitute of the faith that is justifying, have yet other principles in their nature that are capable of giving rise to a great variety of actions both inward and outward, and this as it respects religion and the salvation of their souls. . . . Nor has sin destroyed any of these powers of human nature. . . . Sinners . . . are still capable of thinking, reasoning, considering, and reflecting; they are still capable of chusing some things in preference to others, and of ordering their conduct conformably to such choice . . . a large fund you see is here opened for human endeavours and consequently sinners who have not this faith . . . may yet do a great deal from other principles planted in their nature. And these doings that are . . . spoken of as performed in order to the attainment of it. [*TS*, pp. 202–04]

Chauncy's definition of faith as something lying well within the implanted powers of man fits nicely with his discussions of original sin, the fall, and the image of God. The two requirements for salvation, a moral nature and saving faith, are well within the reach of the man who will take the effort to follow the liberal prescription for salvation and happiness.

Chauncy's intellectualized definition of faith obviously affected the way in which he saw the Scriptures. From the present-day viewpoint it is somewhat ironic that Chauncy the liberal and rationalist was much more literal in his approach to Scripture than were the evangelicals, who are often taken to be the precursors of the modern literalists and fundamentalists. Chauncy attacked the "further light" doctrine of the evangelicals because there is no new light to be expected any more.[18] Rather than look for any further spiritual illumination, he exhorted men to "keep close to the Scripture and admit of nothing for an impression of the SPIRIT but what

---

Princeton theology. On the doctrine of faith at least, the arch-Calvinists of Princeton were one with the founders of Unitarianism.

18. *Enthusiasm Described and Caution'd Against,* pp. 12, 18–20, 100. Hereafter cited in the text of this chapter as *ED*.

agrees with that unerring rule. . . . The Bible is the grand
test by which everything in religion is to be tried" (*ED*, p. 17).

The work of the Spirit, thus subordinated to the Word and
the rational faculties, is only to witness to the Word and to
aid the understanding. (*ED*, pp. 18–20; *TS*, pp. 301–02). The
work of the Spirit

> does not lie, as some may be ready to imagine, in giving
> them new revelations, in suggesting to their tho'ts new
> truths, which the world knew nothing of before; but in
> setting those old truths, which are contained in that
> public, standing, authentic revelation of the divine mind,
> the holy bible, before their view [*TS*, p. 100]

The essentially conservative nature of this liberal theology is
evident. It was this same tendency to subordinate the Spirit
to the Word, to see the Scripture as propositions for assent,
and to define faith in wholly intellectualistic terms that had
moved Continental Calvinism under the leadership of such
men as Wollebius, Voetius, and Turretin in the direction of
Protestant scholasticism. Anglo-Saxon Calvinism, as opposed
to its Continental cousins, preserved more faithfully Calvin's
dialectic of Word and Spirit, mind and heart. With the shatter-
ing of the Puritan synthesis in America at the time of the
awakening, this dialectic was broken. The pole of the dialectic
that emphasized the mind and the literal word came to the
fore both in Puritan liberalism and the scholasticism of nine-
teenth-century Princeton Calvinism, which was based on Continental sources.

This understanding of faith and of the Scriptures also influenced the liberal understanding of the ministry that became
part of the conflict engendered by the Great Awakening. Since
education, according to Chauncy, was the means by which
moral capacities were cultivated and faith arrived at, the most
important prerequisite for the ministry was education. "Can
the minister be this fitted for his office without considerable
Degrees of knowledge?" Chauncy asked rhetorically. No, "his

powers ought to be well cultivated by a good education" (*MC*, p. 14). This was the logical consequence of Chauncy's theology of the Spirit, which subordinated it to reason and the Word.

Chauncy admitted that the Spirit once acted in a more direct way, more in line with the experience of the revivalists. But times had changed.

> The work of the Spirit is different now from what it was in the first days of Christianity. Men were then favoured with the extraordinary presence of the SPIRIT. He came upon them in miraculous gifts and powers. . . . But the SPIRIT is not now to be expected in these ways. [*ED*, p. 16]

Now that Christianity is "settled in the world" there is no need for these direct gifts.[19] Education has replaced the direct action of the Spirit; the ordinary has replaced the extraordinary.

> It will doubtless be said here, the apostles themselves, the first preachers of the Gospel were set of ordinary men, destitute of the advantages of learning. . . . But herein they err, not considering the difference between the State of things now and when the Gospel was first made publick. . . . There is no need of the like extraordinary Influence of the Divine Spirit, now that Christianity has received its confirmation and been established in the world as a Religion coming from God. Accordingly the way of becoming qualified to be Ministers of this religion is not by any miraculous Interposition of Heaven, but by attendence to Reason, Meditation, and Prayer. . . . [The true ministers are] those, who by hard Study, and a considerable stay at the School of the Prophets, have, through a Divine blessing on their endeavours, got their minds furnish't with desirable Measures of Knowledge and Good understanding. There is no room for debate on this matter. [*MC*, pp. 15–16]

19. *The Outpouring of the Holy Ghost*, p. 9.

Now that Harvard University is established, Chauncy told the revivalists, there is no need to try to return to the direct action of God upon the pastor. Things had become more orderly, rational, and predictable, and Chauncy saw no reason to return to more extraordinary times. "The plain truth is, the Spirit of GOD does not assist Ministers now, as in the first days of the Gospel. He did it then by immediate revelation; he does it now in a way more humane, by his blessing on their studies" (*MC*, p. 28).

Chauncy was consistent, and his view of the Spirit and the ministry was all of a piece with the rest of his theology: education was what was necessary to preach the liberal gospel. Chauncy agreed with Gay that ministers are to be teachers of reason and morality.

> Now Christ and his Apostles usually in their preaching addressed themselves to the Reason and Understanding of their hearers: They laid the Matter for Conviction before them in a calm and rational Manner; and thus they treated their hearers as rational creatures; not beginning at first to Work upon their passions and Affections, they used very much Gentleness and Mildness in their preaching.[20]

Thus he assured his readers that, although the Lord and the apostles did not have the "advantages of learning" nor "a considerable stay at the School of the Prophets," they were still good Boston liberals despite their lack of a Harvard M.A. He could then go on to say that "a Great part of Christ's preaching was taken up in explaining Morality and shewing men their obligations," and that ministers ought to do likewise.[21] There was a growing tendency toward moralism in the preaching of the New England Puritans, and Chauncy's almost total concentration on man's moral efforts in salvation in-

20. *The Late Religious Commotion in New England Considered*, p. 23.
21. Ibid., p. 24.

creased the emphasis on the ethical aspects of preaching and the ministry.

Chauncy defined God, the fall, original sin, the image of God, and the nature of the Scripture and the ministry to arrive at a consistent liberal theology. Although much of his work drew upon currents that had already been flowing within American Puritanism, there was one place where a complete break was called for if the benevolence of the deity and the moral worth of man were to be maintained with consistency. As early as the 1750s Chauncy concluded that the idea of eternal punishment could not stand within the system of liberal theology.[22] He set down his conclusion and all the supporting evidence he could muster in a long book entitled *The Mystery Hid from All Ages*. It would not be published for thirty years and then only anonymously.

The ferment that would finally break out into the Revolutionary War was beginning, and Chauncy felt that "men's minds are too much absorbed in politics" to consider the issues in his book. Also, there appeared on the scene John Murray from England, an itinerant evangelist of universalism. Chauncy, not wanting to be associated with him, continued to preach to his congregation as if nothing had changed and never revealed his true opinions. Wrote one friend who knew Chauncy's actual theology:

> Our Saviour said to his followers: "I have many things to tell you, but ye cannot bear them now." And this Dr. C. quotes to excuse his own conduct in concealing his sentiments from the people under his charge, as well as the world in general. [p. 189]

Apparently Chauncy believed in a further light after all. But for thirty years he kept his new light hidden under a bushel and kept up the public pretense of orthodoxy, however liberal,

22. For a description of the development of Chauncy's views of eternal salvation and the controversy they aroused, see Wright, *Beginnings*, chap. 8. The quotations used in the following discussion are all from Wright.

and only in private nurtured his break with the faith of his fathers.

Not until after the Revolutionary War did Chauncy let his closest friends glimpse his manuscript. The clique of Boston liberals began to refer to Chauncy's book by the code name of "the pudding." Thus Chauncy would ask of someone, "Doth he relish the pudding?" to see if it was safe to let him in on the secret. The secret almost came out anyway in one hot debate during a council examining a candidate for ordination that touched on some of the issues raised in the book. Chauncy got very defensive, and one participant wrote that they were almost "obliged to eat the pudding, bag & all." The pretense could not be maintained much longer. In 1872 Chauncy anonymously sent out a preliminary manuscript entitled *Salvation for All Men*. A storm of controversy broke out and the printing presses geared up for another pamphlet war. Although Chauncy had reprimanded the revivalists for provoking controversy and disturbing the order of the churches, his manuscript stirred as much dissension as the awakening. In this overheated atmosphere, Chauncy finally decided to "boil" the pudding. Still seeking to remain hidden behind a facade of anonymity and to conceal his true opinions, the pudding was sent to England for cooking. In 1784 it began to appear, unsigned, in America.

Chauncy's concern was to develop a view of salvation that "reflects most honor on God . . . and is most beneficial to men" (*MH*, p. 15). He wanted to find a definition of God that would make God respected in the eyes of his humanistic contemporaries. Chauncy said the failure to develop such a theology led to deism.

> Nor can I suppose that any soberly thoughtful Deist would ever have recurred to mere reason, in opposition to revelation, for the support of a hope towards God, if he had entertained this idea of its scope and tendency. It is, I am verily persuaded, very much owing to the false light

in which revelation has been placed, and by its very good friends too, that so many have been led to reject it. [*MH*, p. 361]

Perhaps many of Chauncy's own parishioners were turning from revelation after the Revolutionary War, and his attempt to make Christianity more compatible with his age was also an attempt to make it acceptable to his own, increasingly liberal parishioners.

The twin pillars of the new theology for the eighteenth century were, according to Chauncy, the benevolence of the deity and the creation of the world for man's own happiness (*MH*, pp. 1, v). It was the infinitely benevolent God who created the world not for his own glory but for man's own pleasure. "As the first cause of all things is infinitely benevolent, 'tis not easy to conceive, that he should bring mankind into existence, unless he intended to make them finally happy" (*MH*, p. 1). Given the unity of the divine will, God's single intention (to make men happy) was not only the cause of creation and the work of Christ, but also it continued throughout eternity. The divine intention was not merely to make men happy on earth but to make them finally happy. This intention must apply to all men since all men stand in the same relation to God. "There is one God, or more popularly, God is one. That is, all men, reprobate as well as elect, have one and the self same God. . . . So then we see the blessed God stands in the same near and tender relation to the whole human race." [23] Given that God's only intention is to make men happy and that all men stand under this intention, there can only be one conclusion.

Chauncy's way of arguing was not something radically new but stood in direct continuity with his immediate predecessors. All the men considered here grounded creation and redemption wholly in the divine will. Christ's sacrifice had no efficacy

---

23. *Salvation for All Men*, p. 6. Hereafter cited in the text of this chapter as *SAM*.

apart from the divine willingness to accept it and apply it. The reason all men were not saved was not any limitation on Christ's work but only that God did not choose to apply it to all men.

As long as men maintained that God's single purpose was his own glory, it was perfectly possible to base creation and redemption on that purpose and also affirm predestination. God was glorified both by saving some and by damning others. God accepted the sacrifice of Christ and yet did not apply it to all, because he must glorify both his justice (in reprobation) and mercy (in election). When Chauncy redefined God's intention as man's happiness, in order to make the gospel more compatible with his age and his Arminian theology, it was clearly inconsistent to argue that God makes men happy by damning them since damnation was defined as eternal torment. Because God's will was now the expression of his benevolence rather than his glory, universalism was the only possibility. "This will has its ground in the essential benevolence of God's nature. The salvation of all men is good and acceptable in his sight" (*SAM*, p. 5). Redemption remained, as before, grounded in the divine will, but since God's will is benevolence toward men, there is no reason that God should not redeem all. On the contrary, there is every reason that he should. "This mediator gave himself a ransom for all. These words can signify no less than general redemption. . . . Here a price is paid down, such as justice required, and God was pleased to accept" (*SAM*, p. 7). Generations of New England Puritans said that God could have saved all men had he willed it. Chauncy simply said that the benevolence of God entailed that he does will it.

Liberals had often used the fear of hell as a stimulus to morality. Chauncy did not like Murray's arguments for universalism, because they seemed to undercut morality and therefore the whole Arminian soteriology. If all men are to be saved, why does it matter what one does or believes? Chauncy had raised the specter of the antinomians to witness against the revivalists; was it now going to come back and haunt him? In one of those brilliant attempts to keep both the formularies of orthodoxy and the new theology of liberalism, of which Chauncy was clearly capable, he tried to combine the fear of hell with universalism.

Chauncy (and Mayhew) viewed suffering as a stimulus to growth in order to affirm that this was the best of all possible worlds despite the presence of suffering. Applying the same logic to hell, he affirmed there is a hell of suffering, but it is not penal but reformative. "If evil, punishment and misery, in the present life, is mercifully intended for the good of the patients themselves, why not in the next life?" he asked. God's punishment, both in this world and the next, is not intended to show God's justice, but rather it is for "the profit, or advantage, of the sufferers themselves" (*MH*, p. 325). All Puritans affirmed that those whom God loves he also chastises, and some had made this a solution to the problem of evil. Chauncy took this traditional maxim and applied it to hell.

Chauncy continued to emphasize the importance of hell along with his universalism.

> Moral depravity is inconsistent with rational happiness and that it is impossible men should be happy . . . till they are reduced under a willing subjection to the government of God; yea, the reason of their suffering the torments of the next state . . . is that they might be made the willing people of God. [*MH*, p. 343]

It is no wonder that some accused Chauncy of teaching "the Popish doctrine of purgatory." [24] More important is the fact that God's judgment dropped out entirely. Hell was a function of the divine goodness, so there was no need for God's justice. Chauncy developed a doctrine of hell without any taint of a God of judgment.

Chauncy's universalism preserved hell as a stimulus to

24. Samuel Mather, *All Men will not be Saved Forever* (Boston, 1782), p. 8, quoted in Wright, *Beginnings*, p. 192.

moral endeavor. Men were still exhorted to repent and reform or face torment in the next life. They were told to convert and so obtain a happiness in the next life that is denied, at least at first, to the unconverted.

> And the special advantage of believers above other men is, that they are saved from the wrath to come, saved in the next state, and immediately upon the coming of Christ, are admitted to heavenly happiness. Others must stay for this; being unqualified for such felicity they must wait till they are bro't to a better temper of mind. . . . Believers will be roused to everlasting life at Christ's second coming; that unbelievers will be raised too, but only in order to punish them in hell; and that when their punishments shall have produced a proper effect, they will be recovered to the same happiness with the saints. [*SAM,* pp. 8–9]

Those who do not freely choose to undergo the liberal order of salvation in this life will be forced to do so in the next one.

This raises the problem that even Chauncy was never able to solve. Not a new problem, it has been a major focus of this study. Inherited by Chauncy from his Calvinist forefathers, it is the problem of how to balance the divine and human agencies. It is ironic, given Chauncy's assertion of freedom of the will in the face of the Calvinist tradition, that the point at which he deviated most from his fathers is the point at which he encountered the basic problem they had wrestled with. It first appeared that Chauncy simply asserted man's freedom and limited God's sovereignty in order to give room to man's agency and thus fulfill the trend that we have traced through the seventeenth century. But in declaring that it is God's sovereign intention to save all men, he raised the problem of man's freedom in relation to that intention.

> It is not said God would have all to be saved by his good will, but that he authoritatively wills it: wills it as a

being of supreme uncontrolable power, a being that will
be obeyed in spite of the corrupt despositions of men or
the mischievous acts of devils. It is a fixed, determined,
immutable will, not transcient, not revocable. Thus power-
fully and irresistibly does God will all men to be saved.
[*SAM,* pp. 4–5]

God's intention to save all men was asserted with as strong a
Calvinist sense of the sovereignty and irresistibility of God's
power as ever the orthodox asserted God's intention to glorify
himself. Does this mean that the vaunted freedom and moral
agency of man around which Chauncy redefined the whole
Puritan system and upon which he based his relentless controversy with the Edwardsians was at last to be abandoned? He
was faced with a conflict between the twin pillars of his theology—two ideas that he thought ultimately inseparable—the
benevolence of the deity and the autonomy of man. He could
only choose, as any good Calvinist would, divine power over
human agency. God is so benevolent that he will overrule
man's free will to bring him to happiness. Even if men per-
sist in the course of evil, "their creator, being perfectly benevolent, would be disposed to prevent them making or at least
finally persisting in, such wrong choices" (*MH,* p. 2).

We have almost returned to where we began. The problem
of relating the divine sovereignty to human agency gave rise
to the long growth that culminated in Chauncy's theology. In
his last, and what he thought was his most complete, break
with the tradition of his forebears he floundered on the same
rocks that they had sought to avoid by moving in the direction
to which he was heir. He began with an assertion of human
freedom, but by affirming the sovereignty of the divine benevolence in the terms of the strictest Calvinism, he must limit
that human freedom. The essence of eighteenth-century
liberalism was that man could judge for himself what was
best for man and could make God comply with it. Chauncy
concluded by saying that God in his benevolence knows what

is best for man and that he will (as Thomas Shepard said) "compell men to it." One might argue that there is no solution to the problem of balancing the divine and human wills. In the course of this study we have seen several solutions proposed and rejected. Chauncy began with a simple assertion of human freedom and found that, in a universe where God has purposes (however liberal and benevolent) to accomplish, such an assertion was not enough. In the end, in regard to his position on this most central Puritan question, Chauncy died well within the faith of his fathers.

Selected Bibliography of Primary Sources

Ames, William
    1643. *The Marrow of Sacred Theology*. London.
    1658. *Praeparationis peccatoris ad conversionem* in *Disceptatio Scholastica*. Amsterdam.

Briant, Lemuel
    1749. *The Absurdity and Blasphemy of Depretiating Moral Virtue*. Boston.

Bulkeley, Peter
    1651. *The Gospel Covenant: or The Covenant of Grace Opened*. London.

Chauncy, Charles
    1742. *Enthusiasm Described and Cautioned Against*. Boston.
    1742. *The Out-pouring of the Holy Ghost*. Boston.
    1743. *The Late Religious Commotion in New England Considered*. Boston.
    1743. *Seasonable Thoughts on the State of Religion in New England*. Boston.
    1744. *Ministers Cautioned against Occasions of Contempt*. Boston.
    1745. *Marvellous Things Done by the Right Hand and Holy Arm of God in Getting Him the Victory*. Boston.
    1747. *Civil Magistrates Must Be Just*. Boston.
    1758. *The Opinion of One That Has Perused the Summer Mornings Conversation Concerning Original Sin, Wrote by the Rev. Mr. Peter Clark*. Boston.
    1765. *Twelve Sermons*. Boston.
    1782. *Salvation for All Men*. Boston.
    1784. *The Benevolence of the Deity*. Boston.
    1784. *The Mystery Hid from All Ages*. London.
    1785. *Five Dissertations on the Scripture Account of the Fall*. London.

Cleaveland, John
>   1763. *An Essay, to Defend Some of the Most Important Principles.* Boston.

Colman, Benjamin
>   1715. *A Humble Discourse on the Incomprehensibleness of God.* Boston.
>   1716. *A Brief Enquiry.* Boston.
>   1729. *The Credibility of the Christian Doctrine of the Resurrection.* Boston.
>   1735. *A Brief Dissertation on the three first chapters of Genesis.* Boston.
>   1739. *The Unspeakable Gift of God: A Right and Beautiful Spirit.* Boston.
>   1739. *The Wither'd Hand Stretched Forth.* Boston.
>   1740. *Souls Flying to Jesus Christ.* Boston.
>   1741. *The Lord Shall Rejoice in his Works.* Boston.
>   1742. *The Great God Magnified his Word to the Children of Men.* Boston.
>   1743. *The Glory of God in the Firmament of his Power.* Boston.
>   1744. *A Letter from the Reverend Dr. Colman of Boston, to the Reverend Mr. Williams.* Boston.
>   1746. *The Vanity of Man as Mortal.* Boston.

Cotton, John
>   1644. *Sixteene Questions of Serious and Necessary Consequence.* London.
>   1645. *The Covenant of God's Free Grace.* London.
>   1646. *Gospel Conversion.* London.
>   1655. *A Treatise of the Covenant of Grace.* London.

Firmin, Giles
>   1660. *Presbyterial Ordination Vindicated.* London.
>   1670. *The Real Christian.* London.

Gay, Ebenezer
>   1746. *The True Spirit of the Gospel Minister represented and Urged.* Boston.

1747. *The Alienation of Affections from Ministers Consider'd.* Boston.

1743. *Jesus Christ the Wise Master-Builder.* Boston.

1759. *Natural Religion as Distinguished from Revealed.* Boston.

1766. *A Beloved Disciple of Jesus Christ Characterized.* Boston.

1766. *St. John's Vision . . . Explained and Improved.* Boston.

Hooker, Thomas

1638. *The Unbeleevers Preparing for Christ.* London.

1649. *The Covenant of Grace Opened.* London.

1656. *A Comment Upon Christs Last Prayer.* London.

1743. *The Poor Doubting Christian Drawn to Christ.* Boston.

Mather, Cotton

1689. *The Way to Prosperity.* Boston.

1691. *Late Memorable Providences Relating to Witchcraft.* London.

1692. *A Midnight Cry.* Boston.

1693. *The Wonders of the Invisible World.* Boston

1695. *Brontologia Sacra.* London.

1699. *The Faith of the Fathers.* Boston.

1700. *The Resolved Christian.* Boston.

1700. *Reasonable Religion.* Boston.

1702. *Magnalia Christi Americana.* Boston.

1706. *The Good Old Way.* Boston.

1706. *Free Grace Maintained and Improved.* Boston.

1709. *A Christian Conversing with the Great Mystery of Christianity: The Mystery of the Trinity.* Boston.

1712. *Grace Defended.* Boston.

1721. *The Way of Truth Laid Out.* Boston.

1721. *The Christian Philosopher.* Boston.

1727. *Boanerges.* Boston.

1807. *Essays to do Good.* London.

Mayhew, Jonathan
  1750. *A Discourse Concerning Unlimited Submission.* Boston.
  1755. *Sermons.* Boston.
  1755. *The Expected Dissolution of All Things: A Motive to Universal Holiness.* Boston.
  1761. *Striving to enter in at the Strait Gate.* Boston.
  1763. *Two Sermons on the Nature, Extent, and Perfection of the Divine Goodness.* Boston.
  1763. *Christian Sobriety.* Boston.
  1764. *A Letter of Reproof to Mr. John Cleaveland.* Boston.
  1766. *The Snare Broken.* Boston.
Norton, John
  1653. *A Discussion of that Great Point in Divinity: the Sufferings of Christ.* London.
  1654. *The Orthodox Evangelist.* London.
  1659. *The Heart of New-England Rent.* Cambridge.
Perkins, William
  1612, 1613, 1613. *The Works of that Famous and Worthy Minister of Christ, William Perkins.* 3 vols. London.
Shepard, Thomas
  1654. *A Short Catechism.* Cambridge.
  1853. *The Works of Thomas Shepard.* 3 vols. Boston.
Stoddard, Solomon
  1708. *The Falseness of the Hopes of Many Professors.* Boston.
  1709. *An Appeal to the Learned . . . Against Mr. Increase Mather.* Boston.
  1713. *The Efficacy of the Fear of Hell to Restrain Sin.* Boston.
  1714. *A Guide to Christ.* Boston.
  1717. *Three Sermons.* Boston.
  1770. *The Nature of Saving Conversion.* Boston.
Ward, Nathaniel (Theodore de la Guard)
  1647. *The Simple Cobbler of Aggavvam in America.* London.

Willard, Samuel

 1680. *The Duty of a People that have Renewed their Covenant with God.* Boston.

 1682. *Covenant Keeping the Way to Blessedness.* Boston.

 1682. *The Necessity of Sincerity in Renewing Covenant.* Boston.

 1686. *Heavenly Merchandizing.* Boston.

 1693. *The Doctrine of the Covenant of Redemption.* Boston.

 1694. *The Law Established by the Gospel.* Boston.

 1700. *Morality not to be Relied on for Life.* Boston.

 1700. *The Fountain Opened.* Boston.

 1700. *The Peril of the Times Displayed.* Boston.

 1726. *A Compleat Body of Divinity.* Boston.

Index

Age of Reason: Firmin's response to, 50–51; influence on C. Mather, 87–89; Colman's response to, 94–96; and the liberals, 183–84, 191–92

Ames, William, 11, 22–24, 43, 160

Antinomian controversy, 3–11, 138, 156–58, 182

Arminianism. *See* Briant; Chauncy; Gay; Mayhew

Atonement, doctrine of; in Norton, 26–28; in Willard, 61–62; in C. Mather, 79; in Colman, 99; in Mayhew, 152–54

Brattle Street Church, 54, 91–92, 103

Briant, Lemuel: criticized by Stoddard, 119, 120, 122–24; life and thought, 132–38; influence on Mayhew, 142, 146; mentioned, 166, 169

Bulkeley, Peter, 9, 20–22, 41, 64, 72–73

Calvin, John, 11, 13, 30, 87–88

Chauncy, Charles: and universalism, 29, 34, 79, 190–97; and Protestant ethic, 85; and revival, 92; criticized by Stoddard, 115, 120, 124, 127; and Mayhew, 144, 161; life and thought, 165–97

Cleaveland, John, 153–54

Colman, Benjamin: compared with C. Mather, 84, 87–89; life and thought, 90–103; and Brattle Street Church, 144

Conversion: discussed at Antinom-ian Synod, 6–9; according to Norton, 18–26; according to Firmin, 35–37, 40–46, 48; according to Willard, 70–73; according to C. Mather, 81–83; according to Colman, 100–02; according to Stoddard, 111, 113–25; according to Briant, 135–37, 142; according to Mayhew, 154–57; according to Chauncy, 178–86

Cotton, John: influence on Norton, 3–11; in Antinomian controversy, 17–20; rejection of preparation, 23–24, 32, 35; as representative of early Puritanism, 26, 38, 41, 56, 73, 80, 85, 123, 124, 137, 138, 157, 182

Covenant, 21–24, 41, 47–49, 60–64, 71, 80, 86

Deism. *See* Age of Reason

Divine sovereignty: according to Norton, 11–18, 26–29; according to Firmin, 42, 44–45; according to Willard, 58–73; according to C. Mather, 77–83; according to Colman, 93–95; according to Stoddard, 112–13; according to Mayhew, 145–55, 168n 3; according to Chauncy, 166–69, 193–97

Edwards, Jonathan: role in Great Awakening, 34–35, 55, 92, 131–32; in relation to Stoddard, 105, 107–08, 110, 122, 126; dispute with Chauncy, 169–72, 176

Evangelicals. *See* Great Awakening; Edwards; Whitefield

Faith, nature of: discussed at Antinomian Synod, 6, 7–9, 18–20: discussed by Firmin, 41–42, 51; discussed by C. Mather, 82–83; discussed by Stoddard, 115–16; discussed by Chauncy, 182–87

Firmin, Giles, 70–71, 80, 125–126, 138, 154; life and thought, 33–53

Gay, Ebenezer: criticized by Stoddard, 115, 119, 120, 122–24; life and thought, 132–33, 138–42; relation to Mayhew, 143–44, 146, 148; relation to Chauncy, 166, 179

Great Awakening, 34–35, 76, 103, 116–17, 131, 143, 162, 186–89

Hooker, Thomas: role in Antinomian controversy, 3, 10, 12–13, 23, 26; criticized by Firmin, 38, 40, 41, 43, 47, 52; as representative of early Puritanism, 56, 85, 117, 121, 137, 157

Human initiative: according to Norton, 13–18, 20–22, 29–31; according to Perkins, 14–15; according to Firmin, 42–44; according to Willard, 56–58, 65–73; according to C. Mather, 83–86; according to Colman, 94, 99–103; according to Stoddard, 110–16; according to Briant, 135–37; according to Gay, 140–41; according to Mayhew, 150–60; according to Chauncy, 171–86

Hutchinson, Ann. *See* Antinomian controversy

Liberalism. *See* Briant; Chauncy; Gay; Mayhew

Mather, Cotton, 59, 136, 138, 182; life and thought, 76–89; compared with Colman, 90; dispute with Stoddard, 106–07, 125, 127

Mather, Increase: and Harvard College, 55, 91; and Newtonian science, 59, 87; dispute with Stoddard, 105–07, 118, 121, 124

Mayhew, Jonathan: criticized by Stoddard, 124, 126; student of E. Gay, 133; life and thought, 143–64; relation to Chauncy, 166, 170, 179, 194

Natural order: as seen by C. Mather, 87–89; as seen by Colman, 94–99; as seen by Stoddard, 108–09, 112–13; as seen by liberals, 138–40, 146

Newton, Sir Issac, 59, 87, 90, 94–95

Norton, John, 79, 123, 157, 159; life and thought, 3–31; compared with Firmin, 35, 41, 42

Original sin: discussed by Norton, 13–15; discussed by Willard, 68–69; discussed by C. Mather, 81–82; discussed by Colman, 100; discussed by Chauncy, 171–78

Predestination. *See* Divine Sovereignty

Preparation: discussed at Antinomian Synod, 5–7; discussed by Norton, 24; rejected by Firmin, 33–40; revived by Stoddard, 117–22

Princeton theology, 185*n*17, 187

Protestant ethic: in C. Mather, 83–85; in Mayhew, 160–64; in Chauncy, 176–80

Ramus, Peter, 160

Sanctification: at issue in Antinomian controversy, 6; discussed by C. Mather, 83–85; discussed by Briant, 138; discussed by Mayhew, 157–58

Shepard, Thomas: role in Antinomian controversy, 3–4, 9–10, 12–13; relation to Norton, 21–23, 26; criticized by Firmin, 32–33, 36–41, 43, 47, 52; as representative of early Puritanism, 56, 85, 117, 121, 137, 139, 157, 197

Stoddard, Solomon, 91, 154, 157; life and thought, 104–28

Unitarianism, 50–51, 131–32

Universalism, 27–29, 34, 79, 81, 126, 170–71, 190–97

Wesley, John, 157–58

Whitefield, George, 34–35, 92

Willard, Samuel, 138, 149, 182; views on self-interest, 46, 125–27; life and thought, 54–75; compared with C. Mather, 79, 86; supports Colman, 91, 93